Performance-Based Curriculum for Mathematics

From Knowing to Showing

Helen L. Burz
Kit Marshall

Performance-Based Curriculum for Language Arts
Performance-Based Curriculum for Mathematics
Performance-Based Curriculum for Science
Performance-Based Curriculum for Social Studies

Performance-Based Curriculum for Mathematics

From Knowing to Showing

Helen L. Burz
Kit Marshall

CORWIN PRESS, INC.
A Sage Publications Company
Thousand Oaks, California

Copyright © 1996 by Corwin Press, Inc.

For information address:

Corwin Press, Inc.
A Sage Publications Company
2455 Teller Road
Thousand Oaks, California 91320
E-mail: order@corwin.sagepub.com

SAGE Publications Ltd.
6 Bonhill Street
London EC2A 4PU
United Kingdom

SAGE Publications India Pvt. Ltd.
M-32 Market
Greater Kailash I
New Delhi 110 048 India

Printed in the United States of America

Library of Congress Cataloging-in-Publication Data

Burz, Helen L.
    Performance-based curriculum for mathematics: from knowing to showing /
        Helen L. Burz, Kit Marshall.
        p.   cm.
    Includes bibliographical references (pp. 99-100).
    ISBN 0-8039-6495-1 (alk. paper) — ISBN 0-8039-6496-X (alk. paper)
    1. Mathematics — Study and teaching — United States.   2. Curriculum
planning — United States.   3. Competency based education — United States.
I. Marshall, Kit.   II. Title
QA13.B87 1996
510'.71' 273 — dc20   96-12354

This book is printed on acid-free paper.

98 99 00 01 02   10 9 8 7 6 5 4 3 2

TABLE OF CONTENTS

PREFACE

Traditionally, textbooks and curriculum guides have reflected a focus on content coverage. Districts, schools, and educational systems have looked to publishers to define, at least in general terms, *what* should be taught and the order in which it should be taught. The result has been to place an emphasis on what students need to *know*, often with little direction regarding the role of relevance and meaning for the learning.

The impact of technology on society and a scan of future trends clearly deliver the message that just teaching information and "covering the book" are no longer sufficient as a focus for instructional systems. Instead, instruction must go beyond the content taught and actively engage learners in demonstrating how they can select, interpret, use, and share selected information. Educators are quick to accept this shift but are faced with a real need for models that depict ways this might occur.

Performance-Based Curriculum for Mathematics provides a unique model for taking instruction from the traditional focus on content to a student-centered focus that aligns selected content with quality and context.

Because of the focus on content related to a particular content discipline, textbooks and curriculum frameworks and guides have had a strong influence on *how* content is taught. The result, often, has been to teach facts and basic functional skills without using a meaningful, learner-centered approach. There has been no purpose in mind beyond having students know certain information and skills. These previous frameworks and guides have also separated curriculum from instruction and assessment. *Performance-Based Curriculum for Mathematics* offers a new organization and alignment of curriculum, instruction, and assessment around practical classroom application and does it in a way that readily allows teachers to use it.

Although not intended to be a complete daily curriculum guide, *Performance-Based Curriculum for Mathematics* provides a planning framework that includes numerous examples of performance-based mathematics set in real-life contexts. The numerous performance benchmarks, at Grades 3, 5, 8, and 12, and strands can be used directly or as guides for customizing instruction toward relevant and meaningful application of important knowledge around critical mathematical concepts. *Performance-Based Curriculum for Mathematics* can be used to guide the development of mathematics curriculum throughout a family of schools or by individual teachers within one classroom or by an instructional team.

The book is divided into four major sections:

1. Introduction to *Performance-Based Curriculum for Mathematics*
2. The Content/Concept Standards for Mathematics and Performance Benchmarks for 3rd, 5th, 8th, and 12th Grades
3. Technology Connections
4. Performance Designers

The Introduction is organized around a friendly question-and-answer format. This section is central to the planning framework and provides the rationale and organizational structure for the book. The Introduction also contains a discussion of performance-based learning actions.

The Content/Concept Standards for Mathematics represent the best thinking of current national experts and provide the substance for each performance benchmark. These standards are organized by major strands within the discipline. Performance Benchmarks represent descriptions of what could be expected from a student who has a high degree of understanding of a content standard in a high-quality performance. For example, the student might be asked to solve a real-life problem or develop alternative solutions to an issue or question that requires a solid understating of the content/concept standard at one of four developmental levels.

Technology Connections provide guidance for the application of technology in some portion of a performance benchmark. These strategies are appropriate for students who are accessing, producing, and disseminating information through technology.

The last section, Performance Designers, provides an analysis of the performance designer, which is a planning tool for teachers. It requires a focus on the key elements of content, competence, context, and quality criteria.

Finally, design templates and reproducible masters (see Appendix: Blank Templates) provide practical tools that can be used to customize and create classroom instructional material that will empower teachers and students to be successful in "showing what they know."

ABOUT THE AUTHORS

HELEN L. BURZ

Helen L. Burz is a doctoral candidate at Oakland University in Rochester, Michigan, where she received her master of arts degree in teaching. She received her bachelor of science in education from Kent State University. Helen has taught at the preschool, elementary school, and college levels. She has also worked as a principal at the elementary and middle school levels. As an innovative leader in curriculum design and instructional delivery systems, she has led her schools to numerous state and national awards and recognition and was selected as Administrator of the Year in Michigan.

She has addressed integrated curriculum and interdisciplinary instruction for the Association for Supervision and Curriculum Development's (ASCD's) Professional Development Institute since 1985. Currently, she works as an educational consultant across North America speaking and conducting training for future-focused, performance-based curriculum, instruction, and assessment.

KIT MARSHALL

Kit Marshall earned her Ph.D. at Stanford University in educational leadership in 1983 and her master's and BA at Sacramento State University in 1968. After teaching across all levels, developing state and national dissemination grants in innovative educational design, and site-level administration, she pursued further studies in organizational development and technology. She has received numerous awards for her work in restructuring curriculum, instruction, and assessment. Her book, *Teachers Helping Teachers*, published in 1985, was the first practical handbook for educators on team building and mentor teaching.

Currently living in California, Marshall is an international speaker and trainer in future-focused, performance-based curriculum, instruction, and assessment. She is CEO of Action Learning Systems, an educational restructuring company and President of The Learning Edge, a World Wide Web (WWW) site dedicated to networking restructuring schools and communities throughout North America.

INTRODUCTION

Authentic *performance-based education* asks students to take their learning far beyond knowledge and basic skills. A *performance orientation* teaches students to be accountable for knowing what they are learning and why it is important and asks them to apply their knowledge in an observable and measurable *learning performance.*

This shift "from knowing to showing" means that everything we do—instruction, curriculum, assessment, evaluation, and reporting—will ultimately be focused on and organized around these learning performances.

Educators, parents, business and industry leaders, and community members throughout North America are coming to agree that students should be demonstrating what they are learning in observable and meaningful ways. However, we have all been to school. Generally, our collective experience of what school *is* has been very different from what we believe schools need to *become*. If we are to succeed in the difficult shift from content coverage to performance-based education, we will need to have new strategies for defining and organizing what we do around *significant learning performances.*

Performance-Based Curriculum for Mathematics has been developed to provide the tools and the structure for a logical, incremental transition to performance-based education. *Performance-Based Curriculum for Mathematics* is not intended to be a comprehensive curriculum; it is a curriculum framework. The various components of the framework provide structure and a focus that rigorously organizes *content* around *standards* and *performance* around *learning actions.*

IMPORTANT QUESTIONS AND ANSWERS ABOUT *PERFORMANCE-BASED CURRICULUM FOR MATHEMATICS*

Content/Concept Standards

Where do the content/ concept standards come from for this framework?

This framework represents the best thinking of current national experts in the discipline of mathematics. Although there is no official national standard for content areas, the National Council of Teachers of Mathematics (NCTM) has demonstrated strong national leadership and influence that could form the instructional focus in a K–12 mathematics program. These recommendations have been used to form the content/concept foundation of this framework and are identified as content/ concept standards.

How are the content/concept standards organized within this framework?

The discipline of mathematics is organized by major strands within the discipline. These strands are listed and described in Chapter 1. Two of the seven strands are numeration systems and probability and statistics.

How do I know which content/ concept standards to focus on with MY students?

What students should know by the end of four levels, specified as Grades 3, 5, 8, and 12, is described at the beginning of each content Strand section in Chapter 1. These levels are identified to highlight the specific developmental stages the learner moves through in school. A 1st-grade teacher should teach to the development of the concepts identified at Grade 3. A 6th-grade teacher should use the 5th-grade and 8th-grade content/concepts to guide instruction. A 9th-grade or 10th-grade teacher should use the 8th-grade contents as a guide and teach to the 12th-grade content/concepts.

These identified standards provide the content/concept focus for the performance benchmarks within the discipline and within the four developmental levels. Each major strand is identified by a set of content/concepts standards and is followed by four performance benchmark pages: one at each of the four levels—3rd, 5th, 8th and 12th grade.

Performance Benchmarks

What is a performance benchmark?

In *Performance-Based Curriculum for Mathematics*, a performance benchmark is a representative description of what could be expected from a student who has a high degree of understanding of a content standard and can use that content standard in a high-quality performance. For example, the student might be asked to solve a real-life problem or develop alternative solutions to an issue or question that requires a solid understanding of the content/concept standard. If the students don't have the knowledge, they will not do well in the benchmark.

Each performance benchmark is designed to target a particular developmental level identified as 3rd, 5th, 8th and 12th grades. Many students will be able to perform at a higher level and some will perform at a lower level at any given point. Where a student is in the benchmarking process will determine where he or she is in the continuous learning process so characteristic of performance-based education.

What are the components of a performance benchmark?

Each performance benchmark has:

1. A **Key Organizing Question** that provides an initial focus for the performance benchmark and the content/concept standard addressed in the performance benchmark.

2. Performance-based **Key Competences (Learning Actions)** that specify what students need to do with what they know in the performance benchmark (refer to Figure 1.1, The Learning Actions Wheel, on page 6.

3. **Key Concepts and Content** from the discipline that define what students need to know in the performance benchmark.

4. **Two Performance Tasks**, or prompts, that provide the purpose, focus, and authenticity to the performance benchmarks. Having two tasks allows a teacher to ask for a group or individual performance, or even to ask for a repeat performance.

5. **Quality Criteria or "Look fors"** that precisely describe what a student would do to perform at a high-quality level on that performance benchmark. This component serves as the focus for the evaluation process. How well students can demonstrate what is described in the quality criteria informs the evaluator about continuous improvement planning goals for a student. The profile that results from an entire classroom's performance benchmark informs the teacher regarding next steps in the teaching-learning process.

How do I use the performance benchmarks to inform and guide ongoing instruction and assessment?

The performance benchmarks will:

- Organize *what* you teach around a clear set of content/concept standards for a particular discipline

- Organize *how* you teach by focusing your planning on the learning actions that you will teach and assess directly during daily instruction

- Provide you with specific targets for your instruction—you will teach "toward" the performance benchmarks

- Focus your students on what they will need to demonstrate in a formal evaluation of their learning

- Communicate to parents that there is a clear and rigorous academic focus to authentic performance-based education

The performance benchmarks are primarily for evaluation of learning, *after* the learning has occurred. The performance designer, on the other hand, provides the focus for quality continuous improvement *during* the ongoing daily instructional process.

Technology Connections

How about a technology connection for Performance-Based Curriculum for Mathematics?

A number of performance benchmarks in *Performance-Based Curriculum for Mathematics* have a companion application that uses technology in some portion of the performance. If students are currently accessing, producing, and disseminating using technology, you will want to use the strategies found in this section. These technology connections also serve as examples for teachers who are just moving toward the use of technology in their classrooms.

Computer Icon

If there is a computer icon on the performance benchmark page, you can refer to the companion page that will extend the performance benchmark to involve technology.

Performance Designers

What is a performance designer?

A performance designer is an organizer that is used to plan for ongoing performance-based instruction and assessment. The performance designer in *Performance-Based Curriculum for Mathematics* uses the learning actions and connects them to content, context, and criteria. The power of these learning actions becomes apparent when students begin to recognize and improve their competence with each new learning performance.

How is the performance designer used?

The performance designer can be used to organize student performances in any discipline and with students at all developmental levels and in all grades.

The sample performance designers provided can be used just as they are or can serve as a starting point for new designs.

You are invited to copy the blank performance designers in the Appendix for your own classroom use, or you may want to create a new performance designer that fits your style of planning and thinking.

How can I design performances for my students?

Performances can be designed by following the steps provided in Chapter 3 on performance designers.

PERFORMANCE-BASED LEARNING ACTIONS

Learning actions organize what the students will *do* with what they *know* in each performance benchmark. Performance-based learning actions are based on four important beliefs:

1. *Learning is a quality continuous improvement process.*	Students improve their performance with any learning when they have multiple opportunities to apply what they know in a variety of settings over time. As students become familiar with and adept at using certain key learning actions, the quality of each subsequent performance will improve. Students will be *learning how to learn.*

2. *Certain learning actions, or competences, apply to the teaching/learning environment regardless of the age of the learner or the content being taught.*	The five performance-based learning actions coupled with continuous assessment and evaluation are applicable to all ages and in all content areas. The current level of competence with these learning actions will vary from student to student. There will be a considerable range of competence with these learning actions even within a single classroom or grade level. The focus of improvement is on comparison to a learner's last best effort, not comparison of students to one another and not on the content alone. Performance-based teaching and learning will focus on what students can *do* with what they *know.*

3. *Successful people are able to apply certain key actions to every learning challenge. These actions have similar characteristics regardless of the challenge.*	When students learn, apply, and continuously improve in the learning actions, they are practicing for life after they leave school. Schools must allow students to practice for the challenge, choice, and responsibility for results that they will encounter after "life in school" is over. The more competent students are with a range of these learning actions, the more successful they will be in dealing with the diverse issues, problems, and opportunities that await them.

4. *The problem with the future is that it is not what it used to be.*	Today's informational and technological challenges mean that schools must restructure themselves around a different set of assumptions about what students need to *know* and be able to *do.* Many educators and parents are reaching the conclusion that much of the information we ask students to remember and many of the skills we ask them to practice may no longer be appropriate or useful by the time they leave school. At this point, we ask the question, "If covering content is not enough anymore, what *should* schools be focusing on?" We believe the answer is "The learning actions."

THE PERFORMANCE-BASED
LEARNING ACTIONS WHEEL

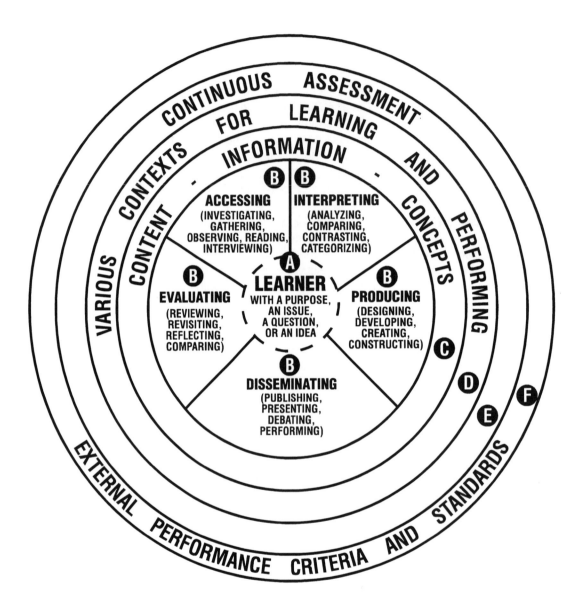

FIGURE 1.1 THE LEARNING ACTIONS WHEEL

Ⓐ The Learner

The learning actions are learner centered and brain based. At the center of the Wheel in Figure 1.1 is the learner with a stimulus for learning. That stimulus may be an issue, idea, or question that may have been suggested to the teacher by the content standards, or it may be something of particular interest to the learner. The learner is in the center because no matter how important we think the content is, it is inert until we add action to it. Everything "revolves" around the developmental levels, the motivation, and the engagement of the learner in the learning actions.

❸ The Five Major Learning Actions of a Performance

The learning actions include five major stages that learners will move through during any performance process. Let's look at the meaning and importance of each.

Accessing

What do I need to know?

How can I find out?

A performance begins with an issue, a problem, or an interesting "lead." The learner accesses the information he or she needs to have in order to successfully perform. This information can come from a variety of experiences—but it must come from somewhere. Traditionally, information has come solely from the teacher or the next chapter in a textbook. In today's information-based environment, students must be adept self-directed learners, determining what is needed and having a wide range of competences for accessing critical information and resources. Learners may investigate, gather, observe, read, and interview, to name a few actions. Whatever actions they engage in to find out what they need to know, *relevant* information must be accessed if the performance is to be as powerful as possible. Accessing is an important first step to a performance and a critical component of success as a learner in any role in or outside school.

Interpreting

What does all of this mean?

So what?

Critical reasoning, problem finding and solving, decision making, and other similar mental processes are what we must do as a part of any important learning that we intend to use in some way. Here, we must make sense of the information we have accessed and decide which information to keep, expand on, or ignore. This component of a performance asks us to analyze, compare, contrast, and categorize—to somehow meaningfully organize the information to represent what we think it all means. This component is critical to a performance process. It clearly determines the level of sophistication and competence with which we can deal with the amount of information constantly vying for our attention and time both in and outside a formal learning situation.

Producing

How can I show what I know?

What impact am I seeking?

Who is my audience?

The producing component of a performance is when we translate what we have learned into a useful representation of our learning. What gets produced represents a learner's competence with design, development, creation, and construction—something tangible that pulls the learning together in some form. This component is the acid test of a learner's competence as a quality producer, a critical role for working and living in the 21st century. In life after school, what we produce usually has a focus, an audience in mind. A powerful performance will always have a clear purpose in mind, a reason for the performance, and an impact that is desired as a result of the performance.

Disseminating

What is the best way to communicate what I have produced?

How can I impact this audience?

How will I know that what I've produced has had an impact?

The fourth learning action of the performance process is disseminating. At this point, we are asking the learners to communicate what they have learned and produced to someone, either directly or indirectly. This is also where the value of an authentic context, someone to be an involved and interested audience, is so apparent. Only in school does there seem to be a lack of attention paid to such a critical motivation for learning and demonstrating. This is truly the point at which learners are dealing with the challenges of a performance setting. Students may publish, present, debate, or perform in a variety of fine and dramatic arts activities, to name a few possibilities. Service learning projects, community performances, and a variety of related school celebrations of learning are all ways for the learning to hold value that may not be inherently present in the simple existence of content standards.

Evaluating

How well did I do?

Where will I focus my plans for improvement?

The evaluation component represents the culmination of one performance and perhaps the launching of another performance cycle. It is the point at which a judgment is made and plans are developed for improvement next time. The quality criteria (in the performance benchmarks) for all the learning actions are the guides for these evaluations. The performance benchmarks in this framework represent the personal evaluation component of ongoing learning and performing on a day-to-day basis.

C Content–Information–Concepts

The learning actions are applied to the content–information–concepts identified by the educational systems as being essential. Addressing information that is organized around major concepts allows the learner to work with a much broader chunk of information, and thus the learner is afforded the opportunity for making more connections and linkages.

In this text the selected information has been aligned with the national standards recommended by the National Council of Teachers of Mathematics.

D Various Contexts for Learning and Performing

A context for learning refers to the setting in which the learning occurs, or the audience or recipient of the fruit of the learning or the situation—any of which create a reason, purpose, or focus for the learning.

Traditionally, the context for learning for students has been alone in a chair at a desk in a classroom. However, the context can be a river or stream that runs through the community. Students working in groups with engineers from a local plant can be engaged in collecting specimens and conducting experiments from the water to determine effects of manufacturing on the water's purity, so they can submit a report to the company or the Environmental Protection Agency.

E Continuous Assessment

The continuous assessment circle of the learning actions wheel represents the continuous improvement process that is imbedded throughout each of the other components. An authentic learning community will engage in a supportive improvement process that is less competitive than it is collaborative and cooperative. To *assess* originally meant "to sit beside." During key points in each component of the performance process, students will reflect upon their own and the work of others. The role of the teacher in this process is to ask questions that guide the student's self-assessment and provide specific feedback to the learner about what is being observed. The conditions we create for this reflective assessment on a daily basis will determine the ultimate success students will have with the performance benchmarks.

F External Performance Criteria and Standards

The outermost circle represents the system's standards and scoring or grading procedures and patterns.

Remember, there are four critical components of a performance. The learning actions represent an organizing tool for a performance. They describe the components of the performance process. The learning actions also represent quality work according to identified criteria. By themselves, the learning actions are of little use. You have to *know* something to *do* something with it. In *Performance-Based Curriculum for Mathematics*, each performance benchmark combines all four components of a performance:

1) Content–information–concepts
2) Competence: learning actions performed by the learner
3) Contexts that create a reason and a focus for the performance
4) Criteria that define a quality performance

1
CONTENT/CONCEPT STANDARDS FOR MATHEMATICS

A MATHEMATICS PERSPECTIVE

As we move into the 21st century, there is consensus among the experts about the necessity for all students to have strong mathematical ability. With this thought in mind, it is imperative that our educational environments provide all students with the opportunities to do worthwhile and purposeful mathematical work. Recognizing and engaging key factors that influence learning—like challenge, motivation, and relevance—it is necessary to provide instructional environments where practices and curricula reflect an integrated approach to problem solving. In such an environment, students must be actively involved in exploration, investigation, and experimentation with models, concrete materials, and everyday objects in order to develop conceptual understanding of mathematical ideas. The future demands that students be involved today in applying higher-order thinking skills to problem-solving situations they can relate to their own experiences and connect directly to real-life examples.

GENERAL MATHEMATICS GOALS

The mission of mathematics instruction is to develop an educational program that will involve, nurture, and enable all students to develop the knowledge and skills they need to function as mature, responsible, and productive citizens in their community, the nation, and the world.

Educational goals for all students, based upon the National Council of Teachers of Mathematics (NCTM) Standards, must reflect the importance of mathematical literacy. Toward this end our goals must be to have students

- Treasure the value of mathematics
- Do and apply mathematics competently
- Find and solve problems
- Communicate mathematically
- Reason mathematically

These goals can be further expanded through the specialized mathematics programs at the following levels.

K–5 Mathematics Curriculum

- The classroom atmosphere fosters the development of logical thinking and problem solving.
- Students use concrete materials regularly in varied activities.
- Students have many opportunities to explore, investigate, and discover.
- Students are continually encouraged to interact with each other to enhance understanding through verbalizing and visualizing.
- Relationships among mathematical skills and concepts are emphasized.
- Students will use computers, calculators, and other forms of technology.

6–8 Mathematics Curriculum

- Previously taught skills are strengthened with a focus on greater depth of understanding in all strands.

- A variety of application assignments are given that incorporate more than one strand and use technology for problem solving.

- More opportunities are provided for thinking independently, solving complex problems, and working in small groups.

- Students are prepared for the more rigorous content and expectations of future learnings.

9–12 Mathematics Curriculum

- Teachers use questioning techniques that create interaction, encourage exploration, enhance transfer, stimulate motivation, and challenge thinking.

- Students are continuously involved in problem-solving activities and are encouraged to solve problems in a variety of ways and accept solutions in many different forms.

- Students investigate, experiment, develop new mathematical skills and concepts, and apply previously acquired knowledge to real-life situations.

CONTENT STRANDS

Because mathematical thinking is an integral part of modern daily life, all students must be exposed to all areas of mathematics to the greatest degree possible and be sufficiently prepared for employment in the workplace or for further study in mathematics and related subjects.

The performance benchmarks presented in this text are influenced by the NCTM Standards and are designed to address the following content strands in mathematics:

- Number sense and estimation

- Numeration systems

- Patterns, relationships, and functions

- Geometry and spatial sense

- Measurement

- Probability and statistics

- Algebraic concepts and operations

CONTENT/CONCEPT STANDARDS

The content/concept standards identified and listed for the four developmental benchmarks are greatly influenced by the work done by the NCTM.

The content presented in the performance benchmarks is not intended to be a complete, detailed list of all information students should know but rather represents essential ideas, concepts, and categories of mathematical information and skills. Educators should consider these examples as a guide for their own selection process as they relate these ideas to locally identified curricula and expectations.

The examples included in this chapter address seven major strands in mathematics. Each of the mathematical strands is identified, briefly described, and then presented in terms of what students should know how to do by the end of Grades 3, 5, 8, and 12. Each strand will be introduced by a listing of the content/concept standards.

PERFORMANCE BENCHMARK FORMAT

The performance benchmarks are sample demonstrations designed with content, competence, context, and criteria that students should accomplish individually and collaboratively by the end of identified grade levels. For each of the seven strands, there will follow four performance benchmarks. There will be one benchmark for each of the following developmental levels: 3rd, 5th, 8th and 12th grade. Because these benchmarks represent different developmental levels, they should serve as guides for all teachers from kindergarten through 12th grade. The performance benchmarks are designed to represent a description of what could be expected from a student in a high-quality performance who has a high degree of understanding of the specific content/concept standard and has consistently experienced the learning actions.

The following template, along with descriptions, is offered as an advance organizer for the performance benchmarks that follow in the next section.

PERFORMANCE BENCHMARK FORMAT

A. MATHEMATICS STRAND AND STANDARD NUMBERS		G. TECHNOLOGY ICON
B. KEY ORGANIZING QUESTION:		
C. KEY COMPETENCES	D. KEY CONCEPTS AND CONTENT	E. PERFORMANCE TASKS
		PERFORMANCE TASK I:
		PERFORMANCE TASK II:
F. QUALITY CRITERIA: "LOOK FORS"		

A. Mathematics Strand and Standard Numbers

This serves to identify the selected mathematics strand and the specific standard numbers chosen from the content/concept standards pages that precede each set of benchmarks.

B. Key Organizing Question

Each performance benchmark addresses specific content information and is organized around a key organizing question. This question serves as a focusing point for the teacher during the performance. The teacher and student can use these questions to focus attention on the key concept/content and competences required in the performance task.

C. Key Competences

The key competences represent the major learning actions of accessing, interpreting, producing, disseminating, and evaluating. These major learning actions are discussed in detail on the preceding pages.

The actions identified are what the student will *do* with the key concepts and content in this benchmark performance. Those do's or learning actions engage students in demonstrations of competence in technical and social processes. Teachers must teach students how to operationalize these learning actions.

D. Key Concepts and Content

The information contained in this section identifies the major concepts that embrace the essential content and knowledge base that was taught and is now addressed in this performance benchmark. These concepts correspond to the standard numbers in Section A above.

E. Performance Tasks

Each performance task requires students to apply the designated content using specific learning actions they have been taught. This is done in a context or situation related to the key question. The performance tasks can be done individually or collaboratively. In either case, it is still the teacher's responsibility to look for the presence or absence of the quality criteria in action.

There are two performance tasks identified on each performance benchmark page to offer teachers a choice or serve as a parallel task for students. Both tasks correspond to the identified quality criteria.

F. Quality Criteria: "Look fors"

The quality criteria represent key actions that students are expected to demonstrate during the performance task. The criteria also guide the teachers and serve as "look fors" during the performance task. In other words, the teacher observes the students for these specific criteria.

These criteria embody the key competences or learning actions that students should have been taught in preparation for this performance task. Students demonstrate the learning actions in connection to the key concepts.

The criteria serve as a process rubric that guides the design of both instruction and assessment. They also serve as a signpost for the learners.

The criteria are identified following a do + what formula, which makes it easy to "look for" them.

G. Technology Icon

The presence of a technology icon at the top of a performance benchmark page means there is a corresponding example in the Technology Connections section. These examples indicate how technologies can assist students in carrying out the key competences required in the performance task.

NUMBER SENSE AND ESTIMATION

Content/Concept Standards

Students must acquire a lasting sense of numbers and number relationships if they are to make sense of the way numbers are used in their everyday world. Students must be able to develop a link between their world and the world of mathematics and recognize the importance of modeling the world around them through mathematical concepts.

What students should know how to do by the end of Grade 3

Students should develop number sense through manipulation of physical objects. They also should recognize that everyday quantitative situations do not always give exact results and that estimation is important in identifying whether or not results are reasonable. They should be able to

1. Connect number sense and numeration to concrete materials
2. Make and use estimations with numbers and measures
3. Apply estimation skills to real-life situations to identify reasonable results

What students should know how to do by the end of Grade 5

Students must develop an estimation mind-set in which they accept estimation as a legitimate and important part of mathematics. They must also recognize that numbers have multiple representations and that it is important to know why a particular representation is useful in a given setting. They should be able to

1. Apply estimation in working with quantities, measurements, computation, and problem solving
2. Recognize when an estimate is appropriate for a situation and apply estimation strategies
3. Interpret the multiple uses of numbers encountered in the real world

What students should know how to do by the end of Grade 8

Through the application of mathematics to other disciplines, students should observe the need for and appropriate use of numbers beyond whole numbers. They should begin to recognize the role of number relationships in developing computational techniques. As they investigate various computational techniques, they should develop an awareness of where and when technology provides an appropriate method of computation. They should be able to

1. Extend their development of number sense to include all real numbers
2. Investigate and appreciate the need for numbers beyond the whole numbers
3. Develop and apply number theory concepts (e.g., primes, factors, multiples) in real-world and mathematical-problem situations
4. Develop, analyze, and explain procedures for computation and techniques for estimation

What students should know how to do by the end of Grade 12

At the high school level, the concepts of number sense and estimation must be expanded to include the use of discrete mathematics as a powerful representation or modeling tool. Students must become aware of the difference between modeling the physical world via continuous mathematics and modeling the world of information systems and data analysis through finite tools such as graphs and matrices. They should be able to

1. Represent problem situations using discrete structures such as finite graphs, matrices, sequences, and recurrence relations
2. Represent and analyze finite graphs using matrices
3. Solve enumeration and finite probability problems

Mathematics:
Grade 3

NUMBER SENSE AND ESTIMATION
CONTENT/CONCEPT STANDARDS 1, 3

KEY ORGANIZING QUESTION:

How can your knowledge of numbers and your ability to estimate help you make decisions that will improve conditions within your school?

KEY COMPETENCES	KEY CONCEPTS AND CONTENT	PERFORMANCE TASKS
Investigate Analyze Create Support	Number sense and estimation: Connect number sense and numeration to concrete materials. Use number sense and estimation to identify reasonable results.	**PERFORMANCE TASK I:** Several students have complained about the lunchroom at school being over-crowded. The principal has asked your team to investigate the situation to see if a problem really exists. Examine the student and lunchroom data given below; create tables, charts, or diagrams to investigate how many people are in the lunchroom; then determine whether you feel the lunchroom is really overcrowded. Write an explanation to support your decision. Student Information: There are 18 classes in the school. There are 22 students in each class. Lunchroom Information: There are 12 tables in the lunchroom. Each table seats 10 students. There are currently 4 lunch periods for teachers to take their classes to. (Students go to lunch with their class. Classes cannot be split.)

QUALITY CRITERIA:
"LOOK FORS"

• Clearly identify the task.
• Identify the important parts of information.
• Select the most appropriate procedures to follow.
• Design a representation.
• Include reasons for your decision and recommendation.

PERFORMANCE TASK II:

If enough new students are added to your school to increase each class to 25 students per class instead of 22, determine how this will affect your decision regarding overcrowding of the lunchroom. Create a new chart or diagram to explain your findings and describe how these additional students affect the situation.

Mathematics:
Grade 5

Performance
Benchmark

NUMBER SENSE AND ESTIMATION
CONTENT/CONCEPT STANDARD 3

KEY ORGANIZING QUESTION:

How could you convince someone that numbers have multiple uses in the real world?

KEY COMPETENCES	KEY CONCEPTS AND CONTENT	PERFORMANCE TASKS
Gather Categorize Write Explain	Number sense and estimation: Interpret the multiple uses of numbers encountered in the real world.	**PERFORMANCE TASK I:** One of the students in your class insists that there is no reason to study mathematics because it has no real use in the outside world. Your teacher has asked you to convince this student that mathematics is used in all aspects of a person's daily life. The teacher has suggested that you use the local newspaper to support your arguments. Gather five examples from the newspaper that can be used to demonstrate the importance of mathematics in daily life. Categorize your examples by the type of mathematics used (e.g., percent, measurement, etc.). Write a statement for each article explaining why you feel it shows how important math is. Present your findings to a team of students. **PERFORMANCE TASK II:** Gather and examine five articles from the newspaper that use mathematics and identify whether they use estimation or exact numbers and calculations. Select one of the articles and explain in a written paragraph why you think estimation was or was not used. Read your paragraph to a team of students and get their reactions.

QUALITY CRITERIA:
"LOOK FORS"

- Select a reasonable amount of varied and appropriate materials.
- Classify and group examples into appropriate sets.
- Select appropriate information to use.
- Organize the information logically and clearly.
- Support your ideas with accurate details.
- Elicit feedback.

Mathematics:
Grade 8

NUMBER SENSE AND ESTIMATION
CONTENT/CONCEPT STANDARDS 1, 4

KEY ORGANIZING QUESTION:

How can you work around the limited options available with high-tech equipment?

KEY COMPETENCES	KEY CONCEPTS AND CONTENT	PERFORMANCE TASKS
Determine Analyze Record Explain	Number sense and estimation: Extend development of number sense to include all real numbers. Develop, analyze, and explain procedures for computation and techniques for estimation.	**PERFORMANCE TASK I:** Your school copying machine has only 3 settings for changing the size of a copy. It can reduce a picture to 77% or 62% of its original size or enlarge it to 120% of its original size. Unfortunately, you have a picture that you need to reduce to 25% of its original size. Determine a method for doing this. Record the steps you took in your process and explain how you arrived at this process.

QUALITY CRITERIA:
"LOOK FORS"

- Review the information and your task.
- Predict possible choices you can make.
- Select the best possibility for accomplishing the task.
- Organize your steps.
- Record your actions and results with clarity and precision.
- Present your reasoning including relevant details.

PERFORMANCE TASK II:
The manufacturer of the copy machine has agreed to add one more setting to the copy machine. If it is a reduction setting, it cannot be less than 40% of the original. If it is an enlargement setting, it cannot be more than 150% of the original. Analyze the reductions and enlargements you needed to make with your group. Select a setting that you feel would be best to add and explain why you made that choice.

Mathematics:
Grade 12

Performance
Benchmark

NUMBER SENSE AND ESTIMATION
CONTENT/CONCEPT STANDARD 1

KEY ORGANIZING QUESTION:

How can airline companies determine the best routes?

KEY COMPETENCES	KEY CONCEPTS AND CONTENT	PERFORMANCE TASKS
Examine Analyze Design Develop Compare Describe	Number sense and estimation/discrete mathematics: Represent problem situations using discrete structures such as finite graphs.	**PERFORMANCE TASK I:** An important use of mathematics is as a representation tool for modeling real-world situations. One such tool is the use of finite graphs to represent problems dealing with scheduling and optimal paths that minimize measures such as cost and distance. The airline industry is highly dependent on mathematical modeling of this nature. Let's consider that a new low-frills airline company has just received permission from the FAA to establish routes as indicated in Table 2.1. Examine the chart and organize the data into an alternative format by developing a finite graph representing all possible routes and the appropriate mileage amounts. Using graph theory methods, compare possible routes from Miami to Los Angeles to find the shortest possible route, and describe how you identified that route.

PERFORMANCE TASK II (continued):

Miami and Los Angeles. Describe that route and explain why it is or is not the same as the route with the shortest distance.

QUALITY CRITERIA:
"LOOK FORS"

• Examine the available data for useful patterns.
• Identify key bits of data.
• Compare and contrast the possibilities.
• Prioritize the information.
• Create a representation.
• Include accurate details.
• Edit according to need.
• Organize ideas according to purpose.
• Present using specific accurate information.

PERFORMANCE TASK II:

As part of their low-frills promotion, an airline company is advertising an innovative pricing structure. All flights of less than 500 miles are offered at a fixed rate of $99 one way. Flights between 500 and 1,000 miles carry a fare of $149 one way. All flights over 1,000 miles are priced at $200 one way. Would you expect that the shortest route would automatically be the least expensive? Create a new one to reflect cost rather than mileage. Use the chart on the following page to determine the least expensive route between

(continues in left column)

TABLE 2.1 AIRLINE DISTANCES TO THE NEAREST MILE

	Boston	New York	Miami	Atlanta	Chicago	Denver	Los Angeles	San Francisco
Boston		191			860			
New York	191		1090	760	722		2451	2576
Miami		1090		595				
Atlanta		760	595		606			
Chicago	860	722		606		908		1855
Denver					908		834	957
Los Angeles		2451				834		349
San Francisco		2576			1855	957	349	

NUMERATION SYSTEMS

Content/Concept Standards

As students investigate numeration systems and their underlying concepts, the central focus should be to empower students with knowledge of the underlying structure of mathematics. Students should begin with concrete experiences and gradually move to more abstract concepts, developing a view of mathematics as a coherent body of knowledge rather than a collection of isolated facts and procedures.

What students should know how to do by the end of Grade 3

Within the study of numeration systems, one important component is recognizing conditions in real-world situations for which a particular operation, or combination of operations, is particularly useful. They should be able to

1. Investigate our number system by relating, counting, grouping, and discovering place-value concepts using concrete materials

2. Develop algorithms, investigate the interrelationships, and apply operations with whole numbers

3. Make mathematical connections between language, symbols, and operations

4. Use manipulatives, role playing, pictures, or models to solve problems using the four basic operations

5. Use models to demonstrate the relationships between fractions, decimals, and whole numbers

6. Use manipulatives to simulate real-life situations that involve fractions and decimals

7. Demonstrate the relevance of mathematical computations to daily-life situations

What students should know how to do by the end of Grade 5

As students expand their knowledge of operations with real numbers, they should explore various methods of computation from paper and pencil to the use of calculators and computers and determine which method is most appropriate for the given situation. They should be able to

1. Investigate meanings for whole numbers, fractions, and decimals through real-world experiences and the use of concrete materials, models, drawings, and diagrams

2. Develop and use comparisons and properties of operations for whole numbers, decimals, and fractions

3. Select and use an appropriate strategy of computing from mental arithmetic, estimation, paper-and-pencil, calculator, and computer methods

4. Compute using the four basic operations on whole numbers, fractions, and decimals

What students should know how to do by the end of Grade 8

By the time students complete middle school, they must have built upon their knowledge of numeration systems to include rational numbers and recognize that rational numbers have multiple representations. In addition, they should also begin to reason proportionally in a variety of real-world settings. They should be able to

1. Represent and use real numbers in a variety of equivalent forms (integer, fraction, decimal, percent, exponential, and scientific notation) in real-world and mathematical-problem situations

2. Apply ratios, proportions, and percents in a wide variety of situations

3. Investigate and use order relations for whole numbers, fractions, decimals, integers, and rational numbers

4. Select and use an appropriate method for computing from mental arithmetic, paper-and-pencil, calculator, and computer methods

5. Compute with whole numbers, fractions, decimals, integers, and rational numbers

What students should know how to do by the end of Grade 12

As students begin to approach the mathematical structure inherent in numeration systems from a more abstract approach, it is important to keep the degree of abstraction or formalism consistent with each student's level of mathematical maturity. Students must also learn to communicate their concepts of structure to others either orally or in writing. They should be able to

1. Illustrate that seemingly different mathematical systems may be essentially the same by using physical materials and models to explore fundamental properties of number systems whenever appropriate

2. Convey a thorough understanding of the real number system including the hierarchy of real numbers, the meaning of infinity, ordering, and basic operations

3. Develop conjecture and intuitive proofs of properties of number systems

4. Demonstrate the logic of algebraic procedures

Mathematics:
Grade 3

NUMERATION SYSTEMS
CONTENT/CONCEPT STANDARDS 2, 7

KEY ORGANIZING QUESTION:

How far can you get on what you know about math?

KEY COMPETENCES	KEY CONCEPTS AND CONTENT	PERFORMANCE TASKS
Investigate Compare Contrast Design Explain	Numeration systems: Apply operations with whole numbers. Demonstrate the relevance of mathematical computations to daily-life situations.	**PERFORMANCE TASK I:** Your class is considering taking a trip by bus this summer. The principal told your teacher that the school cannot afford to have the bus travel more than 600 miles round trip. Use Table 2.2 on the following page which shows miles between several cities your class wants to visit. Investigate several possible trips that would take you to two other cities and back to Washington, DC. Compare the miles each trip takes and design two different trips for your class to choose between. Remember what the principal said about the number of miles. Create a poster to advertise your trips. Explain your choices to the class.

PERFORMANCE TASK II:

Select one of your two trip plans and determine if it matters in which order you visit the two cities. Explain the trip you think is best and why.

Plan another trip that will visit all three cities and determine if it matters in which order you visit the cities. Explain the trip you think is best and why.

QUALITY CRITERIA:
"LOOK FORS"

- Identify your purpose.
- Review the information.
- Examine the data carefully for differences.
- Explore the possibilities.
- Plan a representation.
- Develop a final product.
- Present using accurate details and visuals.

TABLE 2.2 MILEAGE BETWEEN CITIES

	WASHINGTON DC	BALTIMORE	PHILADELPHIA	NEW YORK CITY	BOSTON	ATLANTIC CITY
WASHINGTON DC	0	45	143	237	448	174
BALTIMORE	45	0	102	199	427	136
PHILADELPHIA	143	102	0	101	315	62
NEW YORK CITY	237	199	101	0	222	144
BOSTON	448	427	315	222	0	331
ATLANTIC CITY	174	136	62	144	331	0

Mathematics: Grade 5

NUMERATION SYSTEMS
CONTENT/CONCEPT STANDARDS 3, 4

KEY ORGANIZING QUESTION:

How much math does it take to move the mail?

KEY COMPETENCES	KEY CONCEPTS AND CONTENT	PERFORMANCE TASKS
Identify Summarize Organize Design Create Display	Numeration systems: Select and use an appropriate strategy of computing from mental arithmetic, paper-and-pencil, calculator, and computer methods. Use basic operations for decimal computation.	**PERFORMANCE TASK I:** The post office hasn't always had computers pricing the mail. Not too long ago the clerks would weigh your letter or package, then look up the cost for mailing it on a chart. Every time the postal service had an increase in prices, someone had to recalculate the chart. Suppose you had been working for the postal service B.C. (before computers) and your boss knew that not too far in the future postage was going to rise to our current price of 32¢ for the first ounce and 23¢ for each ounce after that. Because he likes to be prepared, he has asked you to prepare a chart for all the clerks to use when the new pricing comes in. He has told you that clerks must be able to read total cost directly from the chart for all possible weights from 1 ounce to 1 pound, measured in whole-number ounces. The chart must also include prices for international airmail, which he claims will be 95¢ for the first ounce and 39¢ for each half ounce after that. (The airmail chart must be set up in half ounces.) Identify a strategy for calculating the costs, organize the data how you think it should be arranged, calculate the necessary prices, then create the chart.

PERFORMANCE TASK II (continued):

describe a plan for comparing the time it takes to price mail using the chart with the time it takes using technology (either a calculator or a computer). Create a visual to show the difference. Present it to a team of your peers.

QUALITY CRITERIA:
"LOOK FORS"

- Identify the task.
- Select the important details.
- Select the necessary points.
- Condense the information.
- Develop a visual for displaying the findings.
- Create the final accurate product.

PERFORMANCE TASK II:

Not counting the time it took to generate the chart, how efficient do you think this method is compared to using a calculator or computer? Design and

(continues in left column)

Mathematics:
Grade 8

Performance
Benchmark

NUMERATION SYSTEMS
CONTENT/CONCEPT STANDARDS 2, 5

KEY ORGANIZING QUESTION:

How can customers use unit pricing to assist them when purchasing large portions?

KEY COMPETENCES	KEY CONCEPTS AND CONTENT	PERFORMANCE TASKS
Investigate Analyze Calculate Create Display Justify	Numeration systems: Apply ratios and proportions in real-world situations. Compute with whole numbers and decimals.	**PERFORMANCE TASK I:** Have you ever been part of a group of people trying to decide whether to order two medium pizzas or one large? Examine the information below obtained from a local pizza parlor. Identify what "unit" you will use to compare the costs. Decide which information you need to calculate the cost per unit of pizza for various sizes. Determine whether or not the cost is proportional between sizes, and create and display your findings. Discuss whom you think the pricing benefits more, the store or the consumer, and why you think so. Small (9") Medium (12") Large (15") $ 6.49 $ 7.99 $ 9.95

PERFORMANCE TASK II:

If the pizza parlor wants its pricing to be proportional between sizes, predict what price they should charge for their new 24" Mega pizza. Justify your suggested price based on your calculations and any other information you believe is important.

QUALITY CRITERIA:
"LOOK FORS"

• Identify appropriate units.
• Decide what information is needed to determine unit pricing.
• Calculate ratios accurately for unit costs.
• Determine whether costs are proportional based on your calculations.
• Display your findings in a clear and organized manner.
• Discuss the impact of your study using your calculations for support.
• Predict a reasonable pricing structure.
• Justify your prediction based on relevant information.

Mathematics:
Grade 12

NUMERATION SYSTEMS
CONTENT/CONCEPT STANDARD 2

KEY ORGANIZING QUESTION:

How does the structure of our number system allow us to play tricks with numbers?

KEY COMPETENCES	KEY CONCEPTS AND CONTENT	PERFORMANCE TASKS
Interpret Examine Describe Represent Design Assess	Numeration systems: Convey a thorough understanding of the real number system including the hierarchy of real numbers, the meaning of infinity, ordering, and basic operations.	**PERFORMANCE TASK I:** Everyone at some time has seen someone play a number trick where they seem to magically guess what number you are thinking of, or what day your birthday falls on, and many others. Although they appear to be magic, they are readily explained by algebra and mathematical structure. Follow these directions: 1) Select and write down a 4-digit number. 2) Identify and write down the thousands digit. 3) Determine and write down how many hundreds are in the number. 4) Write down the number of tens in the original number. 5) Add those three items. 6) Multiply this result by 9. 7) Calculate the sum of the digits in the original number. 8) Add this sum to the previous product (from Step 6). Examine the resulting number and describe what this trick accomplishes. Examine the steps in this process and illustrate what is actually happening with the numbers by representing the original 4 digits algebraically and constructing each step in the process from an algebraic perspective. What would have to be considered if you were designing a number "trick"?

PERFORMANCE TASK II (continued):

of steps algebraically. Assess whether your trick will look like magic to others or be too obvious. If you feel it is too obvious, modify it to increase the "mystery."

QUALITY CRITERIA:
"LOOK FORS"

• Interpret directions accurately.
• Examine a result to determine its obvious characteristic.
• Clearly describe your observations.
• Examine a process and systematically identify its components.
• Represent (or model) a process using algebraic expressions.
• Design an algorithm that creates an effective number "trick."
• Assess the effectiveness of your trick to appear mystifying.

PERFORMANCE TASK II:

Think of other mathematical magic tricks you have seen, such as guessing age, guessing birth dates, guessing what number you were thinking of, and so on. Design a trick of your own. Illustrate how it works with an example. Describe why it works by representing the sequence

(continues in left column)

PATTERNS, RELATIONSHIPS, AND FUNCTIONS

Content/Concept Standards

Mathematics has been characterized as the language or science of patterns. Pattern recognition and the forming of generalizations are effective problem-solving tools and provide the basis for developing the concept of functions. The study of functions and relationships is further enhanced by the integration of algebra and geometry to provide visual interpretations of patterns, functions, and relationships.

What students should know how to do by the end of Grade 3

Students should be encouraged to look for patterns and relationships as a means of classifying and organizing data. Observing varied representations of a pattern or relationship helps students identify its properties and develop an intuitive idea of functional relationships. They should be able to

1. Investigate, describe, sort, classify, and identify objects and patterns using one or more attributes

2. Analyze the properties of objects to determine relationships and make generalizations

3. Describe, extend, create, and record patterns

4. Investigate the connections among mathematical topics through relationships and patterns in numbers, geometry, and measurement

5. Determine how mathematics applies to the world through relationships and patterns in numbers, geometry, and measurement

What students should know how to do by the end of Grade 5

At this level, work with patterns should still be informal and relatively free of symbolic representation. Students should have the opportunity to generalize and describe patterns and relationships in both numeric and geometric settings. Exploration of patterns should help students build mathematical power and instill in them an awareness of the beauty of mathematics. They should be able to

1. Interpret and create patterns based on the attributes of objects or numbers and validate thinking by using oral and written communication

2. Demonstrate and relate patterns based on the composition and structure of other disciplines (e.g., meter in music, rhythm in poetry, tessellations)

3. Observe, make, and test conjectures by creating examples or constructing counterexamples

4. Solve problems and analyze mathematical situations using patterns and functions

What students should know how to do by the end of Grade 8

In middle school, the study of patterns should begin to shift from informal recognition to a more formal exploration of functions. Students should recognize the importance of using tables, graphs, expressions or equations, and verbal descriptions to generalize and describe patterns and relationships. They also should begin to investigate the dynamic nature of functions in which a change in one variable results in the change of another. They should be able to

1. Describe, extend, analyze, and create a wide variety of patterns

2. Describe and represent relationships with tables, graphs, and rules

3. Generalize patterns using words or symbolic notation

4. Analyze functional relationships to explain how a change in one quantity results in a change in another

5. Make, test, and use generalizations about given information as a means of solving problems and of judging the validity of arguments

6. Represent and solve problems

7. Use technology to explore patterns using patterns and functions

What students should know how to do by the end of Grade 12

At the high school level, the study of patterns and relationships evolves predominantly into the study of functions. Students need to recognize that functions can be represented in a variety of ways such as a written statement, an algebraic formula, a table of values, or a graph and that these representations enable us to model real-world relationships. They should be able to

1. Represent and analyze relationships using tables, rules, equations, and graphs

2. Translate among tabular, symbolic, and graphical representations of functions

3. Model real-life phenomena with a variety of functions

4. Illustrate that a variety of problem situations can be modeled by the same type of function

5. Investigate informally calculus concepts from both a graphical and a numerical perspective

6. Analyze the effects of parameter changes on the graphs of functions through the use of technology

Mathematics:
Grade 3

Performance
Benchmark

PATTERNS, RELATIONSHIPS, AND FUNCTIONS
CONTENT/CONCEPT STANDARDS 1, 2

KEY ORGANIZING QUESTION:

How many ways can you "ADD-vertise"?

KEY COMPETENCES	KEY CONCEPTS AND CONTENT	PERFORMANCE TASKS
Collect Categorize Construct Explain	Patterns, relationships, and functions: Investigate, describe, sort, classify, and identify objects and patterns using one or more attributes. Analyze properties of objects to determine relationships and make generalizations.	**PERFORMANCE TASK I:** How many different types of advertisements have you seen? Do they have anything in common? Are there certain types of items that are advertised more than others? Collect as many different ads as you can from magazines or newspapers. Identify a list of categories so each of your ads belongs to one of those categories. (For example, if someone had an ad for baseball bats, you might want a category titled "sporting goods.") Construct a chart or graph to show how many ads you found of each type. Explain which category seems to be more popular with advertisers.

PERFORMANCE TASK II:

Look at the advertisements printed in a couple of magazines. Identify and categorize at least 10 advertisements according to how they appeal to the reader. Do they use a famous person to sell their product? Do they try to use statistics to make their product better? Do they use some other pattern?

Construct a chart for your advertisements. Present your chart to your class and explain how and why you chose your categories.

*Technology: There are a number of software packages, including some spreadsheets, that will allow students to create their graphs on the computer.

QUALITY CRITERIA:
"LOOK FORS"
- Identify your purpose.
- Collect enough ads to have a wide variety of types.
- Classify ads under well-defined headings.
- Design and develop an accurate display as a chart or graph.
- Present your finding.
- Explain using relevant, accurate information.

Mathematics:
Grade 5

PATTERNS, RELATIONSHIPS, AND FUNCTIONS
CONTENT/CONCEPT STANDARDS 1, 2

KEY ORGANIZING QUESTION:

How do artists and designers use mathematical patterns?

KEY COMPETENCES	KEY CONCEPTS AND CONTENT	PERFORMANCE TASKS
Identify Analyze Create Submit Explain	Patterns, relationships, and functions: Create patterns based on attributes of objects. Demonstrate and relate mathematical patterns within other disciplines.	**PERFORMANCE TASK I:** Tiling patterns or tessellations are commonly used in art or interior design and are a combination of geometric patterns and relationships. The parent committee for your school has raised funds to install a tiled design in the entryway to your school. They want it to be student created and have asked students to submit designs. Identify a geometric figure to use for your design, modify it (making sure it will still tessellate), then create a sample of your tessellation to submit to the class committee for consideration. Explain why you chose this particular shape. **PERFORMANCE TASK II:** Explore combinations of at least two geometric shapes that will result in a pattern that can be tessellated. Create a new design using this combination, and discuss any problems you had by using two shapes instead of one. Materials needed: Pattern blocks or templates for students to trace around or use to plan. *Technology: You could use one of the geometry drawing programs or *Tessellmania* by MECC.

QUALITY CRITERIA:
"LOOK FORS"

- Identify appropriate geometric figures for tessellating.
- Modify the geometric figure to make the tessellation more interesting.
- Create a neat and accurate sample of your tessellation that covers a large enough region for people to visualize the effect.
- Organize your ideas according to purpose.
- Include specific, accurate details.
- Present using concise language.

Mathematics:
Grade 8

PATTERNS, RELATIONSHIPS, AND FUNCTIONS
CONTENT/CONCEPT STANDARDS 2, 4

KEY ORGANIZING QUESTION:

How do the police predict the heights of suspects when all they have is a footprint?

KEY COMPETENCES	KEY CONCEPTS AND CONTENT	PERFORMANCE TASKS
Collect Organize Investigate Analyze Develop Discuss Predict	Patterns, relationships, and functions: Describe and represent relationships with tables and graphs. Analyze functional relationships to explain how a change in one quantity results in a change in another.	**PERFORMANCE TASK I:** Many people believe a mathematical relationship exists between a person's height and the length of his or her foot. In fact, detectives often predict the height of a suspect based on the length of a foot-print. In order to determine if such a relationship really exists, you should create a mathematical model based on data. First you will need to collect data on the height and foot length of many people. Enter the data into a table or into a calculator or computer. Graph it (scatter plot) and describe the relationship between the two quantities. Analyze the way your group collected the data. Discuss any problems that you think may exist in the accuracy of the data. Obtain a foot size from someone not in your data and predict that person's height. Measure the person and see how well you did.

PERFORMANCE TASK II (continued):
tion. Measure the distance and compare with your prediction.
*Technology: You could use a spreadsheet that graphs or a statistical graphing package.

QUALITY CRITERIA:
"LOOK FORS"

• Identify your purpose.
• Gather the necessary data.
• Use a variety of techniques to compare and contrast data.
• Prioritize the most essential findings.
• Arrange the details for viewing.
• Reflect on your process and determine possible problems and possibilities.
• Make a reasonable prediction based on your evidence.

PERFORMANCE TASK II:
Many people believe a mathematical relationship exists between a person's height and how far they can throw a baseball overarm. Collect data on the heights of people and the distance they can throw a baseball. Enter the data into a table. Graph it (scatter plot) and describe the relationship between the two quantities. Analyze your data and discuss any problems that may exist in the accuracy of the data. Obtain the height of a person not in your data collection group. Predict how far that person might throw the baseball based on her height. Let her throw the baseball so you can check your predic-

(continues in left column)

Mathematics:
Grade 12

Performance
Benchmark

PATTERNS, RELATIONSHIPS, AND FUNCTIONS
CONTENT/ CONCEPT STANDARDS 1, 3

KEY ORGANIZING QUESTION:

Do you believe we have a problem with overpopulation in the world? How might we use mathematics to examine this issue as it relates to the United States?

KEY COMPETENCES	KEY CONCEPTS AND CONTENT	PERFORMANCE TASKS
Investigate Analyze Predict Create Explain Justify	Patterns, relationships, and functions: Represent and analyze relationships using tables, equations, and graphs. Model real-life phenomena.	**PERFORMANCE TASK I:** One of the major concerns of people around the world is the trend toward over-population. In order to see if it is a real concern in the U.S., collect data for the United States population over an appropriate period of years. Use technology to model the data and determine what relationship, if any, exists. Based on your analysis, predict what the population will be 10 years from now and justify your prediction. Create a visual to depict your findings. Present and explain it to the group.

QUALITY CRITERIA:
"LOOK FORS"

* Collect accurate, appropriate, and sufficient data.
* Construct a reasonable mathematical model for the data.
* Determine and clearly express the mathematical relationship, if any.
* Make a reasonable prediction.
* Present and explain your findings using appropriate visuals.
* Justify your prediction using appropriate mathematical reasoning.
* Select an appropriate location for investigation.

PERFORMANCE TASK II:
Select either some other country or a particular city of interest in the U.S. for which you can collect population data. Research and organize the data; then mathematically determine and describe the relationship and display your results. Predict the population 20 years from now and justify your prediction. Create a visual to depict your findings. Present and explain it to the group.

Materials needed: *World Almanac Book of Facts* or some other statistical almanac that has population data.

*Technology: Graphing calculators, computer graphing program, or statistics software could be used.

GEOMETRY AND SPATIAL SENSE

Content/Concept Standards

Geometry provides a visual approach to the study of mathematics. Through geometry explorations and investigations, students develop spatial intuitions and an understanding of geometric concepts that are necessary to function effectively in a three-dimensional world. Students should begin their study of geometry by exploring various aspects of the physical world then gradually progressing toward a more abstract level.

What students should know how to do by the end of Grade 3

Students should use manipulative materials to develop geometric concepts and spatial sense. They should first learn to recognize whole shapes and then analyze relevant properties of the shape. They should be able to

1. Investigate, identify, classify, and describe the three-dimensional world in which we live
2. Solve geometric problems using spatial reasoning
3. Investigate and predict the results of combining, subdividing, changing, and transforming shapes

What students should know how to do by the end of Grade 5

Students should continue to use manipulatives as the basis for their development of geometric and spatial sense. Small-group work will encourage developing the ability to use mathematical language to describe real-world phenomena. They should be able to

1. Apply plane and solid geometry vocabulary and ideas to real-life situations
2. Relate geometric concepts to number and measurement ideas
3. Model and construct geometric figures with manipulative materials
4. Identify, describe, classify, and compare geometric shapes, figures, and models
5. Develop spatial sense by learning to visualize and represent geometric figures
6. Explore and predict the results of combining, partitioning, and changing shapes, figures, and models

What students should know how to do by the end of Grade 8

The study of geometry helps students represent and make sense of the world. Students should use geometric models to analyze and solve problems and recognize that geometric interpretations and models can help make an abstract situation more easily understood. They should be able to

1. Identify, describe, compare, and classify geometric figures
2. Illustrate and represent geometric figures with special attention to developing spatial sense
3. Explore transformations of geometric figures
4. Investigate and solve problems using geometric models
5. Apply geometric properties and relationships to solve problems
6. Describe the physical world using geometrical relationships

What students should know how to do by the end of Grade 12

This geometric strand should provide experiences at the high school level that deepen students' understanding of shapes and their properties, with an emphasis on their wide applicability to the real world. Students should have opportunities to visualize and work with three-dimensional figures in order to develop spatial sense fundamental to everyday life and many careers. In addition, the use of models and other real-world objects should aid in the development of geometric intuition that provides a base for working with more abstract ideas. They should be able to

1. Represent problem situations with geometric models and apply geometric properties related to those models

2. Classify figures in terms of congruence and similarity and apply those relationships

3. Deduce properties and relationships between figures from given assumptions

4. Translate between synthetic and coordinate representations

5. Deduce properties of figures using transformations and coordinates

6. Identify congruent and similar figures using transformations

7. Analyze properties of Euclidean transformations and relate translations to vectors

8. Apply trigonometry to problem situations involving triangles

9. Explore periodic real-world phenomena using the sine and cosine functions

Mathematics:
Grade 3

Performance
Benchmark

GEOMETRY AND SPATIAL SENSE
CONTENT/CONCEPT STANDARD 1

KEY ORGANIZING QUESTION:
Where can you find geometric shapes?

KEY COMPETENCES	KEY CONCEPTS AND CONTENT	PERFORMANCE TASKS
Collect Classify Design Create Explain	Geometry and spatial sense: Investigate, identify, classify, and describe the three-dimensional world in which we live.	**PERFORMANCE TASK I:** Geometric shapes occur in many places outside of school. Collect examples of geometric shapes in the real world from photographs, magazines, or newspapers. Classify these pictures by shape and create a display illustrating the shapes you found. Present and explain your display to a partner in another class.

PERFORMANCE TASK II:
Use a variety of geometric shapes to draw a picture that resembles an everyday object. Name the object and identify each shape you used by its geometric name orally or in writing. Create a book of your geometric drawings and explain your drawings to a buddy learner.

QUALITY CRITERIA:
"LOOK FORS"
• Identify your purpose.
• Gather a variety of examples.
• Organize examples according to shape.
• Plan and create a visual depiction of the collected examples.
• Present information and ask for questions.

**Mathematics:
Grade 5**

**Performance
Benchmark**

GEOMETRY AND SPATIAL SENSE
CONTENT/CONCEPT STANDARD 5

KEY ORGANIZING QUESTION:

How can you accurately describe what you see so others can see it too?

KEY COMPETENCES	KEY CONCEPTS AND CONTENT	PERFORMANCE TASKS
Observe Analyze Create Present Review Revise	Geometry and spatial sense: Visualize and represent geometric figures.	**PERFORMANCE TASK I:** Assume one of your friends was not in school yesterday and has called you on the phone to explain the math homework. The homework uses two diagrams that the teacher handed out in class, which your friend does not have. You need to describe these diagrams over the phone so your friend can recreate them on his or her paper. First, identify for your friend whether the drawings show 2-dimensional or 3-dimensional figures. Examine the diagram to determine a clear way to begin. Then write the step-by-step directions you would give to your friend. *(See diagrams in Figure 2.1.)*

PERFORMANCE TASK II (continued):

Wings for Learning and have students match a design and describe how to duplicate an object created by the assembly line.

**QUALITY CRITERIA:
"LOOK FORS"**

• Identify your purpose.
• Identify the essential details.
• Select a sequence for your directions.
• Create a script with necessary details.
• Present your directions to a partner.
• Revise as necessary and try again.

PERFORMANCE TASK II:

What if you were the one who was absent? Interpret the following directions and create the design they describe.

"Create a 5-by-5 grid of dots. Draw a rectangle at the bottom of the grid that is one unit high and four units wide. Now form a triangle above the rectangle by connecting the middle dot in the top row of the grid to each of the upper corners of the rectangle."

*Technology: This performance event could be rewritten to use *The Factory* by

(continues in left column)

FIGURE 2.1 DIAGRAMS FOR
GEOMETRY AND SPATIAL SENSE: GRADE 5

DIAGRAM #1

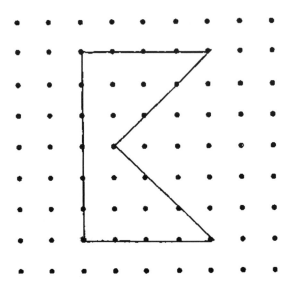

DIAGRAM #2

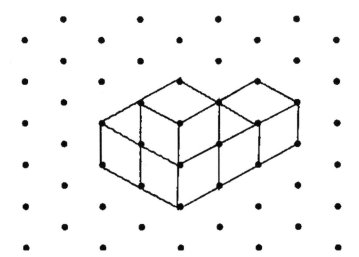

Mathematics:
Grade 8

Performance
Benchmark

GEOMETRY AND SPATIAL SENSE
CONTENT/CONCEPT STANDARD 5

KEY ORGANIZING QUESTION:

How would room size and shape affect the placement of video surveillance cameras?

KEY COMPETENCES	KEY CONCEPTS AND CONTENT	PERFORMANCE TASKS
Investigate Analyze Design Develop Present Justify	Geometry and spatial sense: Apply geometric properties and relationships to solve problems.	**PERFORMANCE TASK I:** A security firm specializes in guarding museums by installing security cameras in each room of the museum. Their closed circuit TV cameras are installed only at corners of the room and continually sweep the room. They install only as many cameras as are needed to observe the entire room. Investigate several rooms shaped like various quadrilaterals to determine whether or not more than one camera is necessary. (Be sure to consider both convex and nonconvex shapes.) Examine the same problem for museums with pentagonal rooms. Determine the best placement for the camera(s) in several of the different room designs that you investigated. Design and develop an illustrated plan depicting the camera placement. Present your plan to a team in your class and explain and justify your decisions.

QUALITY CRITERIA:
"LOOK FORS"

- Investigate a sufficient variety of quadrilateral, pentagonal, and hexagonal room layouts.
- Consider all possible solutions.
- Select your best recommendation.
- Determine successful placements of camera(s).
- Draw appropriate illustrations of room shapes and camera locations.
- Summarize findings in a clear and complete manner.
- Justify your decision with adequate relevant information.
- Describe clearly how you arrived at your solution.

PERFORMANCE TASK II:

Do the number of cameras required to observe the entire room without obstruction change if the museum uses rooms shaped like hexagons? Again, remember the rooms may be convex or nonconvex hexagons. Investigate several room layouts and analyze appropriate locations for cameras. Illustrate the layouts you considered and describe how you determined the number of cameras needed and their locations.

Mathematics:
Grade 12

GEOMETRY AND SPATIAL SENSE
CONTENT/CONCEPT STANDARDS 1, 5

KEY ORGANIZING QUESTION:
Are all wallpaper designs generated by the same basic combinations of geometric patterns? What basic geometry patterns are used to create decorative products? What limitations are there to the patterns?

KEY COMPETENCES	KEY CONCEPTS AND CONTENT	PERFORMANCE TASKS
Select Analyze Design Develop Describe Explain	Geometry and spatial sense: Represent problem situations with geometric models and apply geometric properties and relationships, such as transformations, to those models.	**PERFORMANCE TASK I:** Most wallpaper designs are created by taking a basic picture or pattern then repeating it over and over according to some geometric transformation or series of transformations. Compile several samples of wallpaper designs and analyze them to determine the basic pattern and the transformation or sequence of transformations applied to this pattern in order to generate the complete design. From your analysis, select at least three wallpaper samples that illustrate different transformational processes. For each sample, illustrate and describe the basic pattern and the transformations used. Create a wallpaper design of your own by selecting a basic pattern and applying a series of transformations different from the one you described originally. Explain your design-generating process. Materials needed: an assortment of wallpaper and floorcovering samples that demonstrate several different transformational processes.

PERFORMANCE TASK II (continued):
ering by selecting a basic pattern and applying a series of transformations different from the one you described originally. Explain your design-generating process.

QUALITY CRITERIA:
"LOOK FORS"
- Review an adequate number of samples.
- Compare and contrast designs to determine specific pattern and transformation.
- Select samples illustrating three different transformational processes and describe each clearly.
- Select an idea to develop.
- Represent the idea appropriately.
- Explain your process clearly, including relevant information.

PERFORMANCE TASK II:
You have been asked to create a floor covering design. Review different examples and analyze them to determine the basic pattern in order to generate the complete design. Select at least three samples that illustrate different transformational processes. Illustrate and explain the basic pattern and the transformations used for each sample. Then design and develop your own floor cov-

(continues in left column)

MEASUREMENT

Content/Concept Standards

The measurement strand shows students the usefulness and practical application of mathematics and should provide a strong interaction between students and their environment. As students apply measurement concepts and communicate measurement-related ideas, they should build an awareness of the importance of standard units and common measurement systems.

What students should know how to do by the end of Grade 3

Classroom activities should focus on measuring real objects, making objects of given sizes, and estimating measurements. Initial explorations should involve nonstandard units to which students can easily relate so they will develop some basic understanding of units and begin to recognize the necessity of standard units in order to communicate effectively. They should be able to

1. Estimate, measure, and compare measurable attributes of objects
2. Investigate nonstandard and standard units to measure perimeter, area, volume, and weight
3. Determine the appropriate unit of measurement of time, temperature, and money
4. Create and use measurements to solve problems in everyday situations

What students should know how to do by the end of Grade 5

Measurement concepts such as area, perimeter, time, weight, and so on introduced in earlier grades should be extended and applied to solving problems, exploring the real world, and investigating other areas of mathematics. They should be able to

1. Investigate the concepts of length, capacity, weight, perimeter, area, volume, time, temperature, and angle measurement
2. Use standard (customary and metric) and nonstandard systems of measurement
3. Estimate, construct, and use measurements for description and comparison
4. Select appropriate units and tools to measure to the degree of accuracy required in a particular situation
5. Connect measurement with other aspects of mathematics and with other disciplines

What students should know how to do by the end of Grade 8

As students progress through middle school, they should develop more efficient methods for finding measures and apply formulas to two- and three-dimensional problems. In addition, they should recognize when an estimate is sufficient and what degree of accuracy is required in a given situation. They should be able to

1. Extend their understanding of the process of measurement
2. Estimate, make, and use measurements to describe and compare phenomena
3. Select appropriate units and tools to measure to the degree of accuracy required in a particular situation
4. Increase utilization of systems of measurement
5. Extend their understanding of the concepts of perimeter, area, volume, capacity, weight, and mass

6. Develop the concepts of rates and other derived and indirect measurements
7. Develop formulas and procedures for determining measures to solve problems
8. Solve problems using computation, estimation, and proportions

What students should know how to do by the end of Grade 12

Students need to investigate situations in which measurement plays an important role in everyday life. They need to create an awareness of the need to work with multiple units of measurement and determine accuracy and acceptable degree of error. They should be able to

1. Choose appropriate techniques and tools to measure quantities and apply the relationships between precision, accuracy, and error of measurements
2. Convert measurement units from one form to another and carry out calculations that involve various measurement units
3. Use rates to deal with practical measurement tasks
4. Apply similarity relationships involving length, area, and volume
5. Use suitable methods of approximation to find areas and volumes of irregular shapes
6. Investigate infinite and finite processes involving length, area, and volume
7. Solve problems in two and three dimensions using trigonometric ratios

MATHEMATICS: GRADE 3

PERFORMANCE BENCHMARK

MEASUREMENT
CONTENT/CONCEPT STANDARDS 3, 4

KEY ORGANIZING QUESTION:

How can I design a map others can use?

KEY COMPETENCES	KEY CONCEPTS AND CONTENT	PERFORMANCE TASKS
Explore Compare & Contrast Select Create Distribute Revise Discuss	Measurement: Determine appropriate unit of measurement. Create and use measurements to solve problems in everyday situations.	**PERFORMANCE TASK I:** A class of first graders is planning to visit your school. They will need to find their way from the front door to the cafeteria and then to the library. Think about ways that you can use to describe the distances the children will travel during their visit. Choose the best way and create a map that includes directions and distances. Give another student your map to follow. Reflect on any changes that might make your map better. Create the final product.

QUALITY CRITERIA:
"LOOK FORS"

- Identify your purpose.
- Explore a suitable number of available options.
- Select an appropriate option from those available.
- Create a clear and accurate map.
- Distribute the map to an appropriate user.
- Revise plan appropriately based on feedback.
- Discuss the accuracy of your map using appropriate supporting evidence.

PERFORMANCE TASK II:

A group of parents is planning to visit your school. They will need to find their way from the front door to the auditorium and then to your classroom. Think about ways that you can use to describe the distances the parents will travel during their visit. Choose the best way and create a map that includes directions and distances. How will different tools for measurement (your foot, number of steps, landmarks, tape measures, etc.) affect the accuracy and usability of your directions? Give your map to another student to follow. Reflect on any changes that would improve your map and description before you create a final product.

**Mathematics:
Grade 5**

**Performance
Benchmark**

MEASUREMENT
CONTENT/CONCEPT STANDARDS 1, 3

KEY ORGANIZING QUESTION:

When you only have a certain amount of something, how can you make the most of it?

KEY COMPETENCES	KEY CONCEPTS AND CONTENT	PERFORMANCE TASKS
Identify Review Select Design Explain Justify	Measurement: Investigate perimeter and area. Use measurements for description and comparison; select appropriate units.	**PERFORMANCE TASK I:** Certain cities or neighborhoods require that any dog who is kept outside must be in an enclosed pen. You are planning to get a dog from the animal shelter so you need to design a pen. Someone has given you a 48-foot roll of fencing material. Identify any measurements you need to know or make before designing your pen, then determine the dimensions for a rectangular pen that will give your dog the largest area in which to live, and produce a design on paper illustrating your design with its dimensions. Present your design to the class and explain how you determined what dimensions to use.

**QUALITY CRITERIA:
"LOOK FORS"**

• Identify your purpose.
• Consider the possible options.
• Choose one set of dimensions.
• Create a design accurately marked.
• Explain and justify your design and your process.

PERFORMANCE TASK II:
After you completed the original design for your pen, someone told you that your dog might be better off with an enclosed dog run rather than the pen you had designed. (A dog run means you want a long rectangular pen in which the dog can run in one direction.) Using the same amount of fencing given to you originally, create a new design that gives your dog the longest run possible within the fence. Compare the measurements of the two enclosed areas; decide which pen to build and explain why you made that choice.

Mathematics: Grade 8

Performance Benchmark

MEASUREMENT
CONTENT/CONCEPT STANDARDS 2, 5, 8

KEY ORGANIZING QUESTION:

How can visual models be used to help people interpret measurements?

KEY COMPETENCES	KEY CONCEPTS AND CONTENT	PERFORMANCE TASKS
Listen Identify Estimate Create Reflect	Measurement: Estimate and use measurements to describe and compare phenomena. Extend concept of volume. Use computation and estimation to solve problems.	**PERFORMANCE TASK I:** It has been said that the amount of water used by New York City in one day is approximately one and one-half billion gallons, and that would be equivalent to filling the Empire State Building with water two times. Assume the area of the base of the Empire State building is 87,120 square feet and its height is 1,454 feet. Do you think this would be an accurate visual model? Design a plan for testing this model. Make any necessary calculations and select appropriate units. (Note: 1 cubic foot of water is approximately equivalent to 7.5 gal.) Use your results to either support or disprove the claim about water usage in New York City. Present your findings to your classmates in a visual model with an explanation. **PERFORMANCE TASK II:** Based on the New York example, design a plan for developing a visual display for the amount of water used in Washington, D.C. or any other major city. Identify a building from that city that you feel would be a good model and explain why you chose it. Identify the measurements you would need and how you might get them. In a presentation to the class, describe the procedure you would go through to construct this visual representation and the data you would need for it.

QUALITY CRITERIA:
"LOOK FORS"

- Identify your purpose.
- Estimate volume of a nonstandard container using reasonable estimation methods.
- Check all calculations for accuracy.
- Rehearse your presentation and make any necessary adjustments.

Mathematics:
Grade 12

Performance
Benchmark

MEASUREMENT
CONTENT/CONCEPT STANDARDS 1, 2

KEY ORGANIZING QUESTION:

How can we use mathematics in design and planning?

KEY COMPETENCES	KEY CONCEPTS AND CONTENT	PERFORMANCE TASKS
Identify Determine Calculate Describe Adjust	Measurement: Choose appropriate techniques and tools to measure quantities and apply the relationships between precision, accuracy and error of measurements. Carry out calculations that involve measurement units.	**PERFORMANCE TASK I:** Assume you have been given your first wallpapering job. The room is rectangular and measures 12 feet long by 10 feet wide and is 8 feet tall. There is one door that measures 3 feet wide by 7 feet tall and two windows that are 30 inches wide and 48 inches tall. The wallpaper you have chosen comes in rolls that are 27 inches wide and 34 feet long. The design on the wallpaper repeats itself every 6 inches. First, identify all measurements that you need to consider and determine any other factors that affect the amount of wallpaper needed. Calculate the number of rolls of wallpaper you will need, taking everything into account, and describe the process you used to arrive at that conclusion. (Don't forget that the pattern has to match when you place the strips next to each other on the wall.)

QUALITY CRITERIA:
"LOOK FORS"

- Identify *all* measurements needed to make accurate predictions.
- Determine all factors that will affect the accuracy of your predictions.
- Accurately calculate sufficient amounts taking all factors into consideration.
- Describe the process used in a clear manner with strong justifications for the steps in the process.
- Adjust predictions appropriately based on new information.

PERFORMANCE TASK II:

Like most people, you hung the first strip of wallpaper and decided the color and pattern were all wrong for the room. Luckily the store where you purchased it will take back any unopened rolls. You decide you would rather be out the cost of the one roll rather than live with the wallpaper, so you decide to exchange the wallpaper. However, your new design has a pattern that repeats every 20 inches instead of every 6 inches. Determine whether or not this will affect the number of rolls you need to buy and explain your reasoning.

PROBABILITY AND STATISTICS

Content/Concept Standards

Knowledge of the concepts of probability and statistics is essential to being an informed citizen. With society's expanding use of data for prediction and decision making it is important that students develop an awareness of the concepts and processes used in analyzing data.

What students should know how to do by the end of Grade 3

At this level, activities should be of an investigative or exploratory nature. Students should use actual objects to investigate situations involving chance. They also need to recognize that data comes in many forms and that collecting, organizing, and displaying data can be done in many ways. They should be able to

1. Collect, organize, describe, display, and interpret data
2. Perform, predict, and discuss the outcomes of probability experiments
3. Use data to make decisions and predictions
4. Construct, read, and interpret charts, tables, and graphs

What students should know how to do by the end of Grade 5

Students should actively explore situations by experimentation and simulation. They should use charts, graphs, and plots to reinforce their interpretation of collected data and make predictions. They should be able to

1. Recognize familiar situations that involve change and make simple predictions
2. Use simulations and experiments to determine probabilities (include actual experiments, as well as computer-generated ones)
3. Formulate and solve problems using charts, tables, and graphs
4. Collect, organize, discuss, describe, and make predictions with data
5. Construct, read, and interpret graphic representations of data

What students should know how to do by the end of Grade 8

In order to see how predictions we hear every day are based on probability, students should use their knowledge of probability to solve problems through simulation or modeling. They should build an awareness of the difference between experimental results and the mathematical probability. As they interpret tables and graphs, they should be able to discuss the message conveyed and discuss how changes in the data or in the method of collection might affect the predictions. They should be able to

1. Systematically collect, organize, and describe data
2. Construct, read, and interpret tables, charts, and graphs
3. Make inferences and convincing arguments that are based on data analysis
4. Evaluate arguments that are based on the data analysis
5. Develop an appreciation for statistical methods as powerful means for decision making

6. Model situations by devising and carrying out experiments or simulations to determine probabilities

7. Model situations by constructing a sample space to determine probabilities

8. Appreciate the power of using a probability model by comparing experimental results with mathematical expectations

9. Make predictions and evaluate arguments that are based on the data analysis of experimental or theoretical probability experiments

10. Interpret data using measures of central tendency for data

11. Recognize the pervasive use of probability in the real world

12. Justify the use of sampling and recognize its role in statistical claims

13. Design a statistical experiment to study a problem, conduct the experiment, and interpret and communicate the outcomes

What students should know how to do by the end of Grade 12

The study of probability and statistics in Grades 9-12 should build upon the methods of exploratory data analysis from the elementary and middle grades. Students should be encouraged to apply statistical tools to other academic disciplines and recognize that statistics play an important role in bridging the gap between the exactness of other topics in mathematics and the qualitative nature of a world that is heavily dependent on subjective opinion. They should be able to

1. Explore, compare, and make inferences from single-variable data sets by constructing charts, tables, and graphs, including stem-and-leaf and box plots

2. Summarize and make inferences about single-variable data by applying measures of central tendency, variability, and correlation

3. Look for association in two-variable data by constructing and analyzing fitted lines and smoothing over time

4. Recognize the role of sampling in statistical claims as part of designing a statistical experiment to study a problem, conducting the experiment, and interpreting and communicating the outcomes

5. Compare experimental and theoretical probability, and estimate probabilities from real-world data

6. Use experimental and theoretical probability to represent and solve problems involving uncertainty

7. Create and interpret discrete probability distributions, and describe the normal curve and use its properties to answer questions about sets of data that are assumed to be normally distributed

Mathematics:
Grade 3

Performance
Benchmark

PROBABILITY AND STATISTICS
CONTENT/CONCEPT STANDARDS 1, 2, 4

KEY ORGANIZING QUESTION:

How can mathematics help you to win a game?

KEY COMPETENCES	KEY CONCEPTS AND CONTENT	PERFORMANCE TASKS
Choose Create Predict Conduct Compare Present	Probability and statistics: Collect, organize, and display data in tables. Perform, predict, and discuss the outcomes of probability experiments.	**PERFORMANCE TASK I:** Your school is planning a carnival to raise funds. You know one of the booths will be a game where you guess which way a paper cup will land (bottom up, bottom down, or on its side) if it is tossed in the air. You think you know what the best guess is, but you want to be sure your prediction is correct before you spend money playing the game. You know one way to do this is to conduct an experiment. First, identify how many times you think you should toss the cup in your experiment. Then create a chart showing the three possible ways the cup can land. Keep track of the results of each toss. Before you start, predict how many of your tosses you think will land each way and write it down under your chart. Conduct your experiment and tally the result in your chart for each toss. Compare your predictions to the actual results of the experiment and discuss what the experiment tells you about how to guess at the carnival. Present your findings to another team. **PERFORMANCE TASK II:** There will be a game at the school carnival where you guess in which region the pointer on a spinner will land. The spinner is divided into four regions. Design and conduct an experiment to determine which region is probably the best one to guess. Display the results of your experiment in a chart and discuss how you should guess at the carnival based on those results. Present your findings to another team.

QUALITY CRITERIA:
"LOOK FORS"

• Identify a reasonable number of trials for an experiment.
• Create a recording chart with the correct choices.
• Predict reasonable results.
• Conduct an accurate and orderly experiment.
• Compare predictions to actual results.
• Present your conclusion using supporting data.

Mathematics:
Grade 5

PROBABILITY AND STATISTICS
CONTENT/CONCEPT STANDARDS 2, 4

KEY ORGANIZING QUESTION:

Why are contestants on *Wheel of Fortune* always given R, S, T, L, N, and E as their first letter guesses in the bonus round?

KEY COMPETENCES	KEY CONCEPTS AND CONTENT	PERFORMANCE TASKS
Investigate Analyze Conclude Critique Present	Probability and statistics: Use simulations and experiments to determine probabilities. Collect, organize, discuss, describe, and make predictions with data.	**PERFORMANCE TASK I:** Studies have been done on use of the English language that indicate that the most commonly used consonants are R, S, T, N, and L and the most commonly used vowel is E. Select an adequate number of paragraphs from a variety of sources or use paragraphs given to you. Count the occurrences of these letters and organize your data in a chart or table. Compare and contrast the results of your data collection experiment to the claims of the studies. Based on your conclusions, critique whether the contestants' choice of R, S, T, N, L, and E is a reasonable approach when on the *Wheel of Fortune*. Present your conclusion to another team. **PERFORMANCE TASK II:** Actually, the producers of *Wheel of Fortune* finally changed the rules for the bonus round so they gave every contestant all appearances of R, S, T, N, L, and E in the puzzle prior to starting the bonus round. Then contestants were allowed to pick three more consonants and one more vowel before guessing the word. Analyze letter frequency in the given paragraphs. Use your data to predict one consonant or vowel that contestants should guess in order to have the best chance of selecting a letter that is in the puzzle. Materials needed: Teachers may want to provide sample paragraphs. By doing so it will eliminate having to count letters in every paragraph students provide.

QUALITY CRITERIA:
"LOOK FORS"

• Identify your purpose.
• Select appropriate materials from which to collect data.
• Gather data accurately.
• Organize data in a usable chart.
• Compare and contrast your results with the claims using data from your chart.
• Critique the choice using evidence from your data analysis.
• Organize your ideas and presentation.

Mathematics:
Grade 8

PROBABILITY AND STATISTICS
CONTENT/CONCEPT STANDARDS 6, 7, 9

KEY ORGANIZING QUESTION:

How do advertising promotions affect purchasing habits?

KEY COMPETENCES	KEY CONCEPTS AND CONTENT	PERFORMANCE TASKS
Identify Design Conduct Produce Predict Explain	Probability and statistics: Model situations by devising and carrying out experiments or simulations to determine probabilities. Model situations by constructing a sample space to determine probabilities. Make predictions based on data analysis of experimental probability results.	**PERFORMANCE TASK I:** A major manufacturer of carbonated beverages wants to increase sales by including pictures of rock groups in each carton of their beverage. They plan on using pictures of six different groups. You want to know if it is worth buying cartons to get all six pictures. What are the chances you will really get all six, and how many cartons do you predict you would have to buy? Design a simulation that allows you to conduct an experiment for how many trials it would take to get each of six available items. Identify the "tools" you need for your simulation. Conduct the actual experiment and record results. Make a chart displaying the results of the experiment. Based on those results, predict how many cartons of the product you would most likely need to purchase to get all six pictures. Assess the situation and present why you would or would not choose to participate in this promotional campaign.

PERFORMANCE TASK II (continued):

your chances of getting all seven pictures instead of six. Describe a plan for conducting the new experiment and predict how it might change the results. Present your plan to your team.

QUALITY CRITERIA:
"LOOK FORS"

• Select the necessary components and reasonable tools for a simulation.

• Design a workable simulation.

• Conduct the experiments in an orderly and accurate manner.

• Create a chart that displays accurate and well-organized results.

• Predict what would happen in the real situation based on the simulation results.

• Explain your conclusion appropriately using supporting evidence from the simulation.

PERFORMANCE TASK II:

Beverage sales seem to have improved since this campaign started and the manufacturer wants to improve on what is apparently a good sales technique. They have decided to add a seventh picture to the collection in the hopes they will keep customers who have already received the original six photos. Identify what you would have to change in the original simulation in order to determine

(continues in left column)

Mathematics:
Grade 12

Performance Benchmark

PROBABILITY AND STATISTICS
CONTENT/CONCEPT STANDARDS 1, 2

KEY ORGANIZING QUESTION:

What are some of the ways politicians might use statistics to get elected?

KEY COMPETENCES	KEY CONCEPTS AND CONTENT	PERFORMANCE TASKS
Investigate Analyze Calculate Explain Propose Support Adjust	Probability and statistics: Explore, compare, and make inferences from single-variable data sets by constructing charts, tables, and graphs, including stem-and-leaf and box plots. Summarize and make inferences about single-variable data by applying measures of central tendency and variability.	**PERFORMANCE TASK I:** Political candidates have large staffs of people who analyze data about voters and issues in order to strategically plan their campaign trail. One important factor would be figuring out where the largest concentrations of voters (or would-be voters) are located. Table 2.3 contains some of that information; it lists the number of people (in thousands) who are of voting age by state and by region of the country. Assume you have volunteered to assist a politician who is running for office. You have been asked to put together a visual and verbal display of where the voters are in order to help determine stops along the campaign trail. First identify what type of information or combination of information about the voter population you might want to determine or convey. Then draw comparisons within the data by creating stem-and-leaf plots and box plots. Describe what these plots illustrate about patterns in voter population. Calculate measures of central tendency and variance and explain what these measures tell you about voter population. Propose a plan for the candidate's campaign trail using your analysis of the data as support. **PERFORMANCE TASK II:** Certain states have such high voter populations in comparison to the other states that they might be considered outliers and actually distort the appearance of regional voter population. Identify all states that

PERFORMANCE TASK II (continued):

should be treated as outliers. Adjust your plots and calculations without using these states. Discuss what change, if any, this has on your plan for the campaign trail. Be sure to use your new plots and calculations to support your discussion.

QUALITY CRITERIA:
"LOOK FORS"

- Identify appropriate or usable information to be investigated.
- Compare sections of data by using each type of plot appropriately.
- Create accurate plots.
- Describe reasonable observations from the plots.
- Accurately calculate designated statistical measures.
- Explain clearly what the measurements indicate.
- Propose a logical and workable plan. Support your plan with convincing observations and analysis.
- Adjust data, graphs, and calculations correctly.

(continues in left column)

TABLE 2.3
RESIDENT POPULATION OF VOTING AGE (1990)

NORTHEAST

State	Total*
Maine	924
New Hampshire	835
Vermont	422
Massachusetts	4,646
Rhode Island	776
Connecticut	2,534
New York	13,683
New Jersey	5,927
Pennsylvania	9,091

SOUTH

State	Total*
Delaware	507
Maryland	3,640
District of Columbia	481
Virginia	4,716
West Virginia	1,349
North Carolina	5,061
South Carolina	2,587
Georgia	4,791
Florida	10,180
Kentucky	2,740
Tennessee	3,685
Alabama	2,995
Mississippi	1,832
Arkansas	1,737
Louisiana	2,988
Oklahoma	2,310
Texas	1,222

MIDWEST

State	Total*
Ohio	8,066
Indiana	4,105
Illinois	8,495
Michigan	6,851
Wisconsin	3,616
Minnesota	3,222
Iowa	2,061
Missouri	3,813
North Dakota	462
South Dakota	498
Nebraska	1,152
Kansas	1,819

NORTHEAST

State	Total*
Montana	579
Idaho	707
Wyoming	319
Colorado	2,447
New Mexico	1,075
Arizona	2,696
Utah	1,104
Nevada	929
Washington	3,650
Oregon	2,140
California	22,124
Alaska	382
Hawaii	841

* In Thousands

ALGEBRAIC CONCEPTS AND OPERATIONS

Content/Concept Standards

Algebra as a strand is more than symbolic manipulation of numbers and variables; rather it is a means of representation and a tool for problem solving. As early as elementary school, students should develop a sense of using objects to represent values. Throughout the curriculum, emphasis should be placed on conceptual understanding in addition to facility with symbolic manipulation.

What students should know how to do by the end of Grade 3

Students should begin to form an understanding of the concepts of variables through the use of concrete objects to represent quantities or mathematical relationships. Emphasis should be placed on concepts rather than vocabulary or specific skills. They should be able to

1. Create number stories using manipulatives
2. Demonstrate the use of a symbol to stand for a value
3. Use concrete materials to create algebraic expressions
4. Use open sentences to express mathematical relationships

What students should know how to do by the end of Grade 5

As students begin to bridge the gap between arithmetic and a more formal study of algebra, they must be given opportunities to explore algebraic concepts informally. These explorations should emphasize using physical models, tables, graphs, and other mathematical representations to describe observed physical patterns. Through these explorations students should gain confidence in their ability to abstract relationships from contextual information. They should be able to

1. Use problem-solving strategies to find the values of variables
2. Explore the concepts of variables, expressions, equations, and inequalities
3. Use patterns and relationships to develop and analyze algorithms
4. Explore the use of variables and open sentences to express relationships
5. Apply algebraic methods to solve a variety of real-world and mathematical problems
6. Represent numerical relationships using graphs

What students should know how to do by the end of Grade 8

During middle school, students should build on their informal algebra experiences to begin applying algebraic methods to the solution of real-world problems. They should develop confidence in solving linear equations by formal methods as well as through the use of technology. They should be able to

1. Apply the concepts of variable, expression, and equation
2. Represent situations and number patterns with tables, graphs, rules, and equations and explore the interrelationship of these representations
3. Analyze tables and graphs to identify properties and relationships
4. Develop confidence in solving linear equations using concrete, informal, and formal methods
5. Investigate inequalities and nonlinear equations informally and through the use of technology
6. Apply algebraic methods to solve a variety of real-world and mathematical problems

What students should know how to do by the end of Grade 12

At the 9-12 grade level, students must build on their previous informal exploration of algebraic concepts to begin to appreciate the power of mathematical abstraction and symbolism. Through the use of technology, students can experience a richer set of algebra experiences by allowing them to investigate algebraic models at a conceptual level through representation in terms of graphs, tables, polynomials, and matrices. They should be able to

1. Represent situations that involve variable quantities with expressions, equations, inequalities matrices, and other discrete structures such as sequences

2. Use tables and graphs as tools to interpret expressions, equations, and inequalities, using technology whenever appropriate

3. Evaluate formulas and expressions to solve a variety of applied problems.

4. Perform operations on expressions and matrices and solve equations, inequalities, and systems of equations

5. Recognize the worth, importance, and power of mathematical abstraction and symbolism

Mathematics:
Grade 3

Performance
Benchmark

ALGEBRAIC CONCEPTS AND OPERATIONS
CONTENT/CONCEPT STANDARDS 2, 3

KEY ORGANIZING QUESTION:

How can you get as much as possible for your money?

KEY COMPETENCES	KEY CONCEPTS AND CONTENT	PERFORMANCE TASKS
Identify Organize Draw Select Describe	Algebraic concepts and operations: Demonstrate the use of a symbol to stand for a value. Use concrete materials to create algebraic expressions.	**PERFORMANCE TASK I:** Your class has been asked to prepare grab bags of candy for a school event. The bags will sell for 50¢, but the contents of the bag should be worth 40¢ so the school makes a profit of 10¢ on each bag sold. You can fill the bags with any combination of gumballs and gummy worms. The gumballs are worth 5¢ each and the gummy worms are worth 7¢ each. If the combination of candy you select for a bag is not worth 40¢ exactly, you are to include enough pennies in the bag to make the whole bag worth 40¢. Identify symbols or pictures you will use to represent the items in each bag. Organize several combinations of candy items that are worth 40¢ exactly or almost 40¢. Draw three different bags with their contents. Select one bag that had to have pennies added and describe how you decided how many pennies to add.

QUALITY CRITERIA:
"LOOK FORS"

- Identify your purpose.
- Identify appropriate symbols to represent items.
- Organize several combinations that meet the requirements.
- Draw clear and accurate representations.
- Select an item according to specific criteria.
- Describe accurately how you made your decision.

PERFORMANCE TASK II:

The store where you are getting the candy has decided they will sell you the gumballs for 4¢ and the gummy worms for 6¢ because it is for a school fundraiser. Create three new combinations of candy using the new prices and still making each bag worth 40¢. Draw the bags and their contents and describe any bag that still needs pennies added.

Mathematics:
Grade 5

Performance
Benchmark

ALGEBRAIC CONCEPTS AND OPERATIONS
CONTENT/CONCEPT STANDARDS 4, 5, 6

KEY ORGANIZING QUESTION:

How can mathematics help you prepare for a hoop-a-thon or other fundraising event for charity?

KEY COMPETENCES	KEY CONCEPTS AND CONTENT	PERFORMANCE TASKS
Estimate Describe Develop Create Predict Explain	Algebraic concepts and operations: Explore the use of variables and open sentences to express relationships. Apply algebraic methods to solve real-world problems. Represent numerical relationships using graphs.	**PERFORMANCE TASK I:** A local community organization has decided to hold a hoop-a-thon to raise funds for a local community health clinic. In order to participate, you need to pick up a pledge sheet and get people to pledge a certain amount of money for each basket you make during the hours the hoop-a-thon is held. Before people make pledges, they often ask how many baskets you expect to make and the amount they would owe if you actually make that many. Your job is to create an information sheet for your contributors. Estimate the maximum number of baskets you expect to make. Then write an equation that will tell your donors how much they will owe depending on how much they pledge per basket. Develop and explain a strategy for determining how much a person should pledge per basket if they already know the maximum amount of money they want to end up owing to the event.

QUALITY CRITERIA:
"LOOK FORS"

- Identify your purpose.
- Estimate a reasonable number of baskets.
- Develop an accurate equation representing the situation.
- Describe or illustrate a clear and correct procedure.
- Develop a workable strategy to solve the problem.
- Explain clearly the steps in the problem-solving process.
- Create a graph that is accurate and representative of the possibilities.
- Explain a prediction with substantial supporting information.

PERFORMANCE TASK II:

Assume you ended up collecting $3.50 in total pledges per basket. Create a graph relating the number of baskets you make to the total amount of money you will earn for the health clinic. Be sure to include at least 5 choices for the number of baskets made. Based on your graph, predict whether it is likely that you could earn $150 and explain your reasoning.

*Technology: Spreadsheets could be used as part of this performance event.

Mathematics:
Grade 8

ALGEBRAIC CONCEPTS AND OPERATIONS
CONTENT/CONCEPT STANDARDS 1, 2, 3, 6

KEY ORGANIZING QUESTION:

How big a box can you make from a given piece of cardboard and how can algebra help you know it really is the biggest?

KEY COMPETENCES	KEY CONCEPTS AND CONTENT	PERFORMANCE TASKS
Examine Analyze Create Represent Explain Verify	Algebraic concepts and operations: Apply concepts of variable, expression, and equation. Represent situations and number patterns with tables, rules, and equations. Analyze tables to identify relationships. Apply algebraic methods to solve real-world problems.	**PERFORMANCE TASK I:** A major problem facing manufacturers is designing packages that hold the most amount of their product but use the least amount of packaging material. One way to design a rectangular box for packaging is to take a rectangular piece of cardboard and cut out squares of a given side length x from each corner of the cardboard. Then fold up the side strips to form a 3-dimensional box that will be x units tall. The volume of the box will change depending on the length of the side of the square you cut out. One of your friends has stated that it is obvious that the more you cut out of each corner, the less the box will hold. Another friend thinks that the more you cut out, the more the box will hold because it will be taller. They want you to settle the argument. Given an original sheet of cardboard that measures 16 inches by 20 inches, represent the problem by drawing a diagram and write a formula to calculate the volume of the box that is created by cutting out squares with sides of length x. Create a table of volumes for different values of x. Examine this table to determine what size square should be cut out of the original sheet to create a box with maximum volume. Compare your answer to the statements of your two friends and explain to them why their predictions do or do not work. Present your conclusions.

PERFORMANCE TASK II (continued):

cardboard you used. Select a different size cardboard sheet to start with. Identify the original dimensions of your sheet. Create a volume table for this sheet depending on the size of the square cut out. Verify whether or not your results support the decision you made in the first example and convey your conclusion orally or in writing. *Technology: Spreadsheets could easily be used for this performance event.

QUALITY CRITERIA:
"LOOK FORS"

- Represent the problem with a relevant diagram.
- Write a formula that correctly represents the volume.
- Create an accurate table with an appropriate number of entries.
- Examine the table to accurately determine when the maximum volume occurs.
- Compare results to original predictions.
- Explain differences with enough evidence to be convincing.
- Verify results with supporting evidence.

PERFORMANCE TASK II:

Before trying to convince your friends that your analysis is correct, you realize it may have worked only for the particular size

(continues in left column)

Mathematics: Grade 12

ALGEBRAIC CONCEPTS AND OPERATIONS
CONTENT/CONCEPT STANDARDS 1, 2, 3

KEY ORGANIZING QUESTION:

How much profit do manufacturers make on that recycled paper showing up in your notebooks, shopping bags, and other paper products?

KEY COMPETENCES	KEY CONCEPTS AND CONTENT	PERFORMANCE TASKS
Review Analyze Organize Design Develop Conclude Present Modify	Algebraic concepts and operations: Represent situations that involve variable quantities with equations and inequalities. Use graphs as tools to interpret equations and inequalities, using technology whenever appropriate. Evaluate expressions to solve applied problems.	**PERFORMANCE TASK I:** Recycling paper has become an important part of our country's economic and environmental profile. In addition to helping with environmental concerns, recycling must generate a profit for companies in order for this process to continue. The amount of profit often depends on the proportional amounts of recyclable materials being used in the recycling process. Suppose one of the paper recycling companies uses various combinations of scrap cloth and scrap paper to produce two different grades of recycled paper. You have been working for them part time and would like a full-time job with them. As part of the interview process they want to see how well you apply your mathematics background to solve problems, so they *(continues on next page)*

QUALITY CRITERIA: "LOOK FORS"

- Identify the correct profit function.
- Organize data into appropriate categories.
- Write inequalities accurately representing all constraints.
- Create numerical and graphical representations of the problem.
- Analyze the representations to produce an accurate and reasonable solution.
- Present a realistic recommendation with accurate supporting evidence.
- Modify previous results accurately.
- Compare revised results to original with adequate explanation for any differences.

PERFORMANCE TASK II:

While you were preparing your report, the company found out that their anticipated supply of recycled paper will be cut from 800 pounds to 700 pounds. Modify your previous calculations and graphs to reflect this change. Compare your new results with those you obtained originally. Describe what effect, if any, this change will have on the amount of each grade of paper the company should produce to still maximize their profit.

*Technology: This event would lend itself very well to use of graphing calculators or computer graphing packages.

Mathematics: Grade 12 continued

ALGEBRAIC CONCEPTS AND OPERATIONS
CONTENT/CONCEPT STANDARDS 1, 2, 3

KEY ORGANIZING QUESTION:

See previous page.

KEY COMPETENCES	KEY CONCEPTS AND CONTENT	PERFORMANCE TASKS
See previous page.	*See previous page.*	**PERFORMANCE TASK I (continued):** *Continued from previous page.*

have asked you to review the following information and present a conclusion regarding how much of each grade of recycled paper they should produce to maximize their profit.

"A single batch of Grade A paper requires 30 pounds of scrap cloth and 180 pounds of scrap paper. A single batch of Grade B paper requires 15 pounds of scrap cloth and 160 pounds of scrap paper. The company has on hand 100 pounds of scrap cloth and 800 pounds of scrap paper. The profit from Grade A recycled paper is $450 per batch, whereas Grade B paper yields a profit of $275 per batch."

Identify the profit function to be maximized. Organize the data given to you and write inequalities representing the constraints. Analyze the problem by creating graphs, solving equations, and evaluating expressions either manually or by using appropriate technology. Summarize your results and present your recommendation for the company.

QUALITY CRITERIA: "LOOK FORS"

See previous page.

PERFORMANCE TASK II:

See previous page.

2
TECHNOLOGY CONNECTIONS

SUMMARY

Why Address Technology in a Performance-Based Curriculum?

A performance-based curriculum starts with the understanding that students will make use of what they learn in the production and dissemination of knowledge. Technology is revolutionizing the way we access information; the capabilities we have in interpreting and analyzing data; the methods by which we produce, design, and construct products resulting from our learning; the forms those products take; the methods by which the products are disseminated; and the evaluation procedures we can undertake. Access, interpret, produce, disseminate, and evaluate: these are the five central learning actions in a performance-based curriculum. These learning actions used in conjunction with technology give the learner more power and lead to greater effectiveness.

Technology as Content

Our physical, social, and material worlds are being radically changed as a result of the explosion of new technologies. Technological change

PERFORMANCE-BASED LEARNING ACTIONS WHEEL

and the issues stemming from that change provide content that is increasingly addressed in the study of history, economics, political science, and other disciplines making up the social sciences. They are also subject matter for novels, science fiction, and political and social essays. Technology is a central focus of futuristic studies. It is a product of, as well as a critical ingredient in, modern science. Technological developments have radically altered the tools used by authors and everyone involved in communication and the use of language. Technology is a rich source of topics for integrating a performance-based curriculum.

Technology as a Tool

Technology is also used as a tool in a performance-based curriculum. Although technology can be used as a way of controlling the learner's interaction with the curriculum, technology is most appropriately used as a tool controlled by the learner in the performance-based approach to learning. It is that approach that is applied in correlating this section with the Mathematics section.

Many technologies can enhance a performance-based curriculum. Their common characteristic is that they are tools that improve communication of and access to multimedia data (words, numbers, sounds, still and motion pictures, still and motion graphics) and make the use of those data easier and more effective. In a perfect world, every student and teacher would have a workstation equipped with a computer, modem, CD-ROM, laserdisc player, and a videotape camera and player. This workstation would be connected to networks that allow access to multimedia data on demand. The networks would distribute information in multimedia format to others throughout the world. In addition to these workstations, teachers and learners would have access to copying, scanning, and printing machines; CD-ROM presses; video editing equipment; audio recording and editing equipment; and software to support writing, computer-aided design, statistics, graphing, musical and artistic productions, and so on. Additional equipment would be found in a science laboratory, including tools for specialized data collection and analysis. In other specialty areas, such as art, lithographic presses would be available. Drafting equipment, electronic tools, and other specialized technologies would be present where necessary to allow the teaching of those technological subject areas.

Technology is a tool (among other tools) useful for acquiring, storing, manipulating, and communicating information in a multimedia format. Technology can be used to gather data, explore questions, produce products, and communicate results.

Technology in Support of Learning Actions

Five learning actions are central to a performance-based curriculum: **ACCESS, INTERPRET, PRODUCE, DISSEMINATE, AND EVALUATE.** Throughout this curriculum framework, the use of appropriate technologies will support students in being active learners. Students will be encouraged to use technology to generate questions and identify problems in a wide variety of contexts; formulate hypotheses and generate tentative solutions to the questions or the problems they have defined; test the reasonableness of their answers and respond to challenges to their positions; reach a conclusion about an issue, a problem, or a question and use that "solution" as a jumping-off place to ask other questions; and engage in the learning process again.

A learner with a purpose, an issue, a question, or an idea needs to be able to use appropriate technologies in carrying out these learning actions. Technology is especially important in accessing information, producing products, and disseminating the results of one's work. We organize the benchmarks of the skills students must have in using technology around these key learning actions that can take full advantage of current technologies: **ACCESS, PRODUCE,** and **DISSEMINATE.** Examples have been developed for two strands of each of the grade levels in mathematics. Each example contains suggestions on how to use technology to **ACCESS** information, **PRODUCE** products, and **DISSEMINATE** the results of one's efforts. These examples are meant to stimulate and facilitate the mastery of the use of appropriate technologies in the pursuit of learning. The suggested technologies encompass a broad range of tools useful in accessing, producing, and disseminating data that are not just words and numbers but are also sounds, still and motion graphics, and still and motion pictures. Students and teachers are encouraged to use all appropriate tools and disseminate their products using a combination of technologies.

Technology changes rapidly. The skills and abilities described below require modification on a regular basis to reflect the latest technologies. These skills and abilities must be understood as dynamic objectives rather than as static goals. They are essential learning actions that increase the student's ability to **ACCESS, PRODUCE,** and **DISSEMINATE.**

SKILLS AND ABILITIES

How students should be able to use technology by the end of Grade 3

Access:

A1	Gather information with still, digital, or video camera
A2	Search databases to locate information
A3	Gather sounds and conversations with audio and video recorders
A4	Collect digitized audio data
A5	Access information on laserdisc by using bar code reader
A6	Scan to capture graphic data
A7	Copy to gather graphics
A8	Retrieve and print information using a computer
A9	Gather information through telephone
A10	Select and use information from CDs
A11	Fax to send and receive printed information
A12	Identify and use all types of materials, such as print, nonprint, and electronic media
A13	Locate information using electronic indexes or media

Produce:

P1	Draw and paint graphics and pictures using a computer
P2	Create flip card animations using a computer
P3	Design and develop computer products including pictures, text, flip card animations, sounds, and graphics
P4	Design and develop audiotapes
P5	Design and develop videotapes
P6	Create overhead or slide presentations with or without background music
P7	Develop stories using computer-generated text with either handmade or computer-generated illustrations

Disseminate:

D1	Present *Logo* or *HyperCard* (or similar) computer product including pictures, text, flip card animations, sounds, and graphics
D2	Publish printed page including text and graphics
D3	Broadcast audiotape
D4	Broadcast videotape
D5	Present overhead or slide presentation
D6	Fax information to other audiences
D7	Explain products or creations to an audience

How students should be able to use technology by the end of Grade 5

Access:

A1   Gather information with a still, digital, or video camera of moderate complexity

A2   Gather information using text-based databases to locate information

A3   Access information on laserdisc by using bar code reader and computer controls

A4   Gather information using telephone and modem to connect to other users and databases (Internet, eWorld, etc.)

A5   Search basic library technologies for data

A6   Select and use specialized tools appropriate to grade level and subject matter

A7   Record interviews with experts

A8   Scan CD collections for needed information

Produce:

P1   Create path-based animations using computer

P2   Create with computer painting and drawing tools of moderate complexity

P3   Digitize still and motion pictures

P4   Create basic spreadsheet for addition, subtraction, multiplication, and division

P5   Graph data (pie charts, line and bar graphs) using computer

P6   Create edited videotapes of moderate complexity using a videotape editing deck or computer-based digital editing system or two connected cassette recorders (VCRs)

P7   Input text into computer using keyboard with appropriate keyboard skills

P8   Design and develop moderately complex *Logo* or *HyperCard* (or similar) programs including pictures, sounds, flip card and path-based animations, graphics, text, and motion pictures

P9   Design and develop multipage document including text and graphics using computer

P10   Create edited audiotape

P11   Create edited videotape

P12   Create overhead or slide presentation with synchronized voice narration with or without background music

P13   Lay out advertisements, posters, and banners

Disseminate:

D1   Present moderately complex *Logo* or *HyperCard* (or similar) computer product including pictures, sounds, flip card and path-based animations, graphics, text, and motion pictures

D2   Publish multipage printed document including formatted, paginated text and graphics

D3   Broadcast edited audiotape and videotape

D4   Present programs using overhead projector, slide projector, or computer

D5   Present information over public address system in a school, community, or meeting situation

D6   Display information in a variety of formats

D7   Advertise for events, services, or products

D8   Broadcast performances and products

D9   Broadcast on cable TV

How students should be able to use technology by the end of Grade 8

Access:

A1   Gather information using computer, CD-ROM, and laserdisc databases

A2   Gather data using telephone and modem (including graphics and sounds) to and from other users and databases (Internet, eWorld, etc.)

A3   Search basic spreadsheet and databasing software for "what if?" comparisons and analyses

A4   Search technologies for accessing data outside the school and local library

A5   Search menus to locate information on computer software, CD-ROM, or laserdiscs

A6   Video interviews

A7   Download information from Internet

Produce:

P1   Create products using computer painting and drawing tools, including moderately complex color tools

P2   Digitize still and motion pictures

P3   Create edited videotapes by using a videotape editing deck or computer-based digital editing system

P4   Create computer presentation program

P5   Develop cell-based animations using computer

P6   Design and develop complex *Logo* or *HyperCard* (or similar) programs including still pictures; flip card, path-based, and cell-based animations; sounds; graphics; and motion pictures

P7   Create multipage documents including text and graphics using computer page layout tools

P8   Develop audiotapes that combine sounds and voice data from a variety of sources

P9   Produce videotapes that are organized, coherent, and well edited

P10   Create a personal database requiring the collection of data over time

Disseminate:

D1   Present relatively complex *Logo* or *HyperCard* (or similar) product including still pictures; flip card, path-based, and cell-based animations; sounds; graphics; and motion pictures

D2   Publish multipage printed documents including text and graphics

D3   Broadcast edited audiotape of moderate complexity

D4   Broadcast edited videotape of moderate complexity

D5   Broadcast video presentation over schoolwide Channel 1 (Whittle), citywide public Channel 28, or citywide ITFS schools-only equipment

D6   Advertise events, services, or products

D7   Display information and designs on various formats available

D8   Broadcast on closed circuit or cable television

D9   Broadcast filmed and live performances on television

D10   Distribute over available sources in Internet

How students should be able to use technology by the end of Grade 12

Access:

A1   Access and use complex electronic databases and communication networks of all types including, but not limited to, Internet

A2   Research using sensors, probes, and other specialized scientific tools as appropriate

A3   Gather information from spreadsheet, databasing software, and statistical packages, including the use of formulas and charting routines

A4   Search technologies for data and primary sources (publications and persons)

A5   Identify local, regional, and national databases and procedures for needed data

A6   Review online bulletin boards, databases, and electronic retrieval services for data

Produce:

P1   Create with complex computer painting and drawing tools and programs

P2   Create 3-D using drawing and modeling tools

P3   Create changing images using computer digital-morphing programs

P4   Illustrate concrete and abstract concepts using computer-aided design and mathematical modeling

P5   Create CD-ROM simulations

P6   Create complex cell-based animations, including 3-D objects, using the computer

P7   Create complex *Logo* or *HyperCard* (or similar) programs including pictures; flipcard, path-based, and cell-based animations; sounds; 3-D graphics; and motion pictures

P8   Develop multipage documents with information from a variety of sources, including text and graphics using appropriate computer page layout tools

P9   Create documents using a variety of fonts and type faces

P10   Assemble findings based on spreadsheets, databasing software, and statistical packages involving the use of formulas as appropriate

P11   Design graphic and text titles for digital video productions

P12   Develop digitally edited materials including audio, motion pictures, still-frame pictures, motion graphics, and still-frame graphics

P13   Design and develop a personal database of moderate complexity

P14   Illustrate concrete and abstract mathematical and scientific concepts

P15   Assemble information by creating, searching, and sorting database

P16   Design and develop a dissemination design for video using ITFS microwave and satellite up-and-down links

Disseminate:

D1   Transmit complex *Logo* or *HyperCard* (or similar) computer product including pictures; flip card, path-based, and cell-based animations; sounds; 3-D graphics; and motion pictures

D2   Publish multipage printed documents, appropriately laid out, including text and graphics

D3   Transmit complex spreadsheet or database findings

D4   Telecast digital video product of some complexity

D5   Present computer-based animation program (cell- or path-based animations, or both)

D6   Publish reports generated from database searches

D7   Publish scientific investigations and results or recommendations

D8   Transmit a video presentation to secondary students using ITFS microwave, Whittle Channel 1 equipment, public Channel 28, cable hookups, and satellite up-and-down links to local schools or students in other school systems

Technology Connections
Mathematics: Grade 3

GEOMETRY AND SPATIAL SENSE
CORRESPONDING PERFORMANCE BENCHMARK, PAGE 36

KEY ORGANIZING QUESTION:

Where can you find geometric shapes?

ACCESS	PRODUCE	DISSEMINATE
PERFORMANCE TASK I: Copy examples of geometric shapes from pictures in your computer, or scan in pictures of examples of geometric shapes that you collect.	**PERFORMANCE TASK I:** Using a painting or drawing program, or a word processor, arrange by geometric shape the pictures you have scanned or gathered. Label each classification.	**PERFORMANCE TASK I:** Print your document and create a display or puzzle for younger students to find the shapes in classrooms and around the school. You can fax your puzzle to students in another school.
PERFORMANCE TASK II: Look through some of your favorite picture books and locate examples of how the illustrator has incorporated the use of geometric shapes in the illustrations.	**PERFORMANCE TASK II:** Design a series of pictures using a computer program like *Desktop Publishing* or *Microsoft Publisher*. Make sure your pictures contain a variety of geometric shapes. You might even create a story about your pictures.	**PERFORMANCE TASK II:** Print your document and create a book that you can share with other students.

GEOMETRY AND SPATIAL SENSE
CORRESPONDING PERFORMANCE BENCHMARK, PAGE 37

KEY ORGANIZING QUESTION:

How can you accurately describe what you see so others can see it too?

ACCESS	PRODUCE	DISSEMINATE
PERFORMANCE TASK I: Have your partner sit at the computer using the computer's paint or draw program. Do not let your partner see the object at which you are looking. For this exercise you should use a two dimensional object. Also have a tape recorder set up to record your descriptions and any reactions your partner may have.	**PERFORMANCE TASK I:** As you describe the object you are observing, your partner should be drawing the object on the computer. When he or she has completed the drawing, listen to the tape recording while looking at the completed drawing. Digitize your recorded instructions. Break your instructions into parts. Using *HyperCard* or *Logo*, or some similar program, create separate pages or cards showing what was added to the drawing at each stage. Attach your digitized instructions to each card or page and have those instructions play as the viewer watches the changes that were made as a result of those instructions.	**PERFORMANCE TASK I:** Play the program linking the drawing with your instructions. Discuss why the instructions did or did not lead to an accurate rendition of the object being considered. After completing the project, switch places with your partner and repeat the exercise.
PERFORMANCE TASK II: Using a word processor, list the steps necessary to draw a two-dimensional object chosen by you.	**PERFORMANCE TASK II:** Have your tester follow your instructions and, using the computer's draw or paint program, draw the object following the directions you have given. You may also want to be the drawer and let your partner be the instructor offering a new set of directions.	**PERFORMANCE TASK II:** Print the drawing done by your tester. Discuss why the results were or were not what you expected. Repeat the exercise with a different object. Send the list of instructions to a distant partner over the modem. Have your distant partner send his or her drawing back to you. Communicate over the network discussing why the results were or were not like those you expected.

**Technology Connections
Mathematics: Grade 8**

GEOMETRY AND SPATIAL SENSE
CORRESPONDING PERFORMANCE BENCHMARK, PAGE 39

KEY ORGANIZING QUESTION:
How would room size and shape affect the placement of video surveillance cameras?

ACCESS	PRODUCE	DISSEMINATE
PERFORMANCE TASK I: You are a member of a security team asked to identify appropriate placement of surveillance cameras in various rooms in a building. In preparation for designing a surveillance plan, using a video camera, determine the range and angle of view of the camera at various distances. Record these data. Collect these data with the camera in rooms of varying sizes and shapes.	**PERFORMANCE TASK I:** Using what you have learned about cameras, convex and non-convex shapes, and relationships to space, create a plan using appropriate computer tools. Include scaled space, quantity of cameras needed, and placement of cameras in your plan.	**PERFORMANCE TASK I:** Print your drawings. Make sure the number of cameras, as well as their placement, are clearly specified on your drawings. Present your drawings to another team and ask them to do a critique as representatives of a security firm.
PERFORMANCE TASK II: You are a member of a security team asked to identify the appropriate placement of surveillance equipment on the outside of a house. Choose a house design or picture. Using a video camera, determine the range and angle of view of the camera at various locations. Record your data.	**PERFORMANCE TASK II:** Using your collected information and knowledge, design and develop a plan for your home security coverage. Include scaled space and camera locations for your house surveillance plan.	**PERFORMANCE TASK II:** Print your plan. Check to make sure you have complete surveillance. Present your plan to another team and ask for their input and suggestions.

**Technology Connections
Mathematics: Grade 12**

**Performance
Benchmark**

GEOMETRY AND SPATIAL SENSE
CORRESPONDING PERFORMANCE BENCHMARK, PAGE 40

KEY ORGANIZING QUESTION:
Are all wallpaper designs generated by the same combinations of geometric patterns? What basic geometry patterns are used to create decorative products? What limitations are there to the patterns?

ACCESS	PRODUCE	DISSEMINATE
PERFORMANCE TASK I: You are a wallpaper designer who has been commissioned to design different but complementary wallpapers for three different rooms in one house. Review different existing wallpaper patterns. Select one and scan it into the computer. Use it to develop new variations or create your own wallpaper patterns using your selected combination of geometric patterns.	**PERFORMANCE TASK I:** Your client wants the design to vary while maintaining the same basic pattern in all three rooms. Using appropriate painting or drawing tools, create three versions of the same basic pattern.	**PERFORMANCE TASK I:** Produce your designs. Create a display of your wallpaper designs and include a generated description for the client using a word-processing package. Describe how the pattern was developed including its various transformations. Be sure to create titles for the three transformations.
PERFORMANCE TASK II: You have been asked to teach a mathematics lesson for sixth graders on the use of geometric form in architecture. Using resources available through your computer, gather information on the design of the Sydney Opera House in Sydney, Australia designed by Jorn Utzon.	**PERFORMANCE TASK II:** Use the basic design of the west side of the Sydney Opera House and design a lesson on geometric patterns for the sixth graders. Use a computer-generated diagram of the Opera House that the sixth-grade students could use in their learning experience. Be sure to address line segments, arcs, angles, vertex, congruent shapes, and planes as they explore the use of geometric patterns in architectural design. Have them use the computer to explore these concepts.	**PERFORMANCE TASK II:** Present and teach your lesson on the use of geometric form in architecture to a group of sixth graders. Be sure you begin by asking pertinent questions to get them to tell you what they know about geometric patterns, architecture, and the Sydney Opera House. Engage them in the discovery process using technology. Listen carefully to clarify their questions, and check for understanding when you are done.

**Technology Connections
Mathematics: Grade 3**

**Performance
Benchmark**

MEASUREMENT

CORRESPONDING PERFORMANCE BENCHMARK, PAGE 43

KEY ORGANIZING QUESTION:

How can I design a map others can use?

ACCESS	PRODUCE	DISSEMINATE
PERFORMANCE TASK I: Gather information on maps and nonstandard units of measure. Select a usable unit of measure.	**PERFORMANCE TASK I:** Using the drawing or paint tools, draw a map that visitors to your school could use to find several locations in your school. Clearly identify each of those locations on your map. Indicate the distances on your map using the nonstandard unit of measurement that your group agreed on.	**PERFORMANCE TASK I:** Print your map and photocopy it for use when visitors come to your school. Include a questionnaire to give to users of the map to find out how useful your map was and how you might be able to improve it.
PERFORMANCE TASK II: Review information from a CD-ROM source on nonstandard units of measure and also maps.	**PERFORMANCE TASK II:** Using the drawing or paint tools, or a program on simple maps, draw a map of your home. Clearly identify important locations. Indicate on your map the distance from the kitchen to another room in your house using a nonstandard unit of measure.	**PERFORMANCE TASK II:** Print your map and make a photocopy. Ask a member of your family or a close friend to use your map and give you feedback on it.

Technology Connections
Mathematics: Grade 5

**Performance
Benchmark**

MEASUREMENT

CORRESPONDING PERFORMANCE BENCHMARK, PAGE 44

KEY ORGANIZING QUESTION:

When you only have a certain amount of something, how can you make the most of it?

ACCESS	PRODUCE	DISSEMINATE
PERFORMANCE TASK I: Gather information from the CD-ROM encyclopedia on dog pens or kennels.	**PERFORMANCE TASK I:** Using the drawing tools of the computer, produce a design for a dog pen that uses 36 feet of fencing. Clearly label your drawing with the measurements of your design. Provide a descriptive paragraph that tells why this design would be good for the dog.	**PERFORMANCE TASK I:** Print a copy of the drawing of the proposed pen for the dog. Also print a copy of the paragraph that explains your reasoning. Create a poster and present it to your class.
PERFORMANCE TASK II: You have a 20 m length of fence to enclose a rectangular section of prairie. How many different rectangular designs can you get with the 20 m fence? Which rectangles have the greatest area?	**PERFORMANCE TASK II:** Use *Mathkeys,* a software program. Use the electronic tiles found in *Unlocking Geometry.* Create as many versions of rectangles as you can using the 20 m of fencing. Create a chart using a spreadsheet to account for all of the possibilities and organize all of the dimensions.	**PERFORMANCE TASK II:** Print out your example. Also print a copy of your chart. Present your findings to another team. Compare your findings with theirs.

**Technology Connections
Mathematics: Grade 8**

**Performance
Benchmark**

MEASUREMENT
CORRESPONDING PERFORMANCE BENCHMARK, PAGE 45

KEY ORGANIZING QUESTION:

How can visual models be used to help people interpret measurements?

ACCESS	PRODUCE	DISSEMINATE
PERFORMANCE TASK I: Using a spreadsheet, or other appropriate computer tool, calculate how much water could be held in the building you have selected if it were a closed container. Use your CD-ROM to locate a clear picture of a well-known public building or monument. Get the dimensions on them.	**PERFORMANCE TASK I:** Using a digital camera, take a picture of some object associated with water such as a water faucet. Digitize that picture into your computer. Create a drawing of your building as a closed container. Using flip-card animation techniques, or an animation program, create a visually attractive program showing your building filling with water. Using the building or buildings you have drawn and the digitized picture that you took, create an animated program calling attention to the amount of water being used in your city.	**PERFORMANCE TASK I:** Present your program to a senior math class. Ask for responses from your viewers about the effectiveness of your animated display in drawing attention to water usage in your city.
PERFORMANCE TASK II: Gather the necessary information you will need or estimate how much water is used in your house or apartment each month.	**PERFORMANCE TASK II:** Create an animated program, using *LOGO, HyperCard,* or other appropriate tools, to illustrate the water usage in your house or apartment during one month. In your animated display or program, compare the usage of water in your residence to some familiar object. (For example, would your water usage fill a bathtub or a car?)	**PERFORMANCE TASK II:** Present and explain your program to another math class. Ask for responses from your viewers about the effectiveness of your animated display in drawing attention to water usage in houses or apartments in your city.

**Technology Connections
Mathematics: Grade 12**

**Performance
Benchmark**

MEASUREMENT
CORRESPONDING PERFORMANCE BENCHMARK, PAGE 46

KEY ORGANIZING QUESTION:

How can we use mathematics in design and planning?

ACCESS	PRODUCE	DISSEMINATE
PERFORMANCE TASK I: Using a random number generator in *HyperCard, Logo,* or any other computer program with that capability available to you, generate a width for a room between 12 feet and 20 feet in whole numbers. Generate a number for the length of the room between 14 feet and 24 feet. You have been told that you are to wallpaper the room. In addition to the length and width of the room that you have generated using a random number generator, you know that the room is 8 feet tall. The room has two windows that are 32 inches wide and 48 inches tall. There is one door that is 3 feet wide and 7 feet tall. The design on the wallpaper repeats itself every 6 inches. The patterns must match when you put the wallpaper on the walls. The rolls of wallpaper are 34 feet long and 27 inches wide. You are to calculate the number of rolls you need to wallpaper the room. **PERFORMANCE TASK II:** Same as Performance Task I.	**PERFORMANCE TASK I:** Produce a spreadsheet. Clearly identify all relevant measurements in your calculations. Calculate the number of rolls of wallpaper you will need. Will this spreadsheet work for any size room? Generate a new set of random numbers and see what happens if you change the length, width, or both. Will the spreadsheet work if you add more windows? Another door? The repeat length of the pattern? If not, produce a spreadsheet that will work under all of the conditions specified. **PERFORMANCE TASK II:** Calculate the number of rolls necessary if the pattern repeats every 20 inches instead of every 6 inches. If you originally purchased wallpaper that came in the same length rolls and the same width, but the pattern repeated every 6 inches instead of 20, would you have bought more or fewer rolls of wallpaper? Be sure that your spreadsheet can be clearly understood by others.	**PERFORMANCE TASK I:** Print your spreadsheet. Present and explain your spreadsheet including examples to another student or team and ask for their reactions and suggestions. **PERFORMANCE TASK II:** Present and explain your spread sheet to another design team. Ask them to critique your work and offer suggestions.

**Technology Connections
Mathematics: Grade 12**

**Performance
Benchmark**

PATTERNS, RELATIONSHIPS, AND FUNCTIONS

CORRESPONDING PERFORMANCE BENCHMARK, PAGE 33

KEY ORGANIZING QUESTION:

Do you believe we have a problem with overpopulation in the world? How might we use mathematics to examine this issue as it relates to the United States?

ACCESS	PRODUCE	DISSEMINATE
PERFORMANCE TASK I: Locate a digitized map of the United States in a database. Locate population data for the United States in a database (CD-ROM, laserdisc, or network as appropriate). Collect data for a variety of categories. Enter your data for the United States population over an appropriate period of years into a database program, a spreadsheet, or a statistics package.	**PERFORMANCE TASK I:** Create a graph or graphs of the population trends as shown in your data for your selected categories. Predict the population in 10 years and include your prediction (clearly identified as such) in a revised chart or graph. Animate your chart or graph.	**PERFORMANCE TASK I:** Present your animation and distribute it and the data to at least one other person over a computer network. Ask for their reaction and response. What could you do to improve your animation?
PERFORMANCE TASK II: Locate a digitized map of the country or city selected for this exercise in a database. Locate data for the selected city or country in a digital database (CD-ROM, laserdisc, or network). What are the population patterns for several different categories and regions? Enter data for the selected country or city into a database program, a spreadsheet, or a statistics package.	**PERFORMANCE TASK II:** Create a graph or graphs of the population trends as shown in your data for your selected categories. Predict the population in 10 years and include your prediction (clearly identified as such) in a revised chart or graph. Animate your chart or graph.	**PERFORMANCE TASK II:** Present your animation and distribute it and the data to at least one other person over a computer network. Ask for their reaction and response. What could you do to improve your animation?

3
PERFORMANCE DESIGNERS

The ultimate key to success with performance-based education is the creativity, rigor, and consistency of focus that must characterize the ongoing instructional process in the classroom. Student success with the performance benchmarks identified in this text depends on daily interactions with the learning actions. Students must feel empowered to demonstrate the learning actions being taught so they can internalize them, take ownership, and apply them easily in the benchmark performances. They must be able to do this through a continuous improvement process with a focus on quality criteria.

In order to accomplish the performance benchmarks in this text, learners must have daily practice with the routine of learning and demonstrating through learning actions as they gain new understanding about concepts from the different disciplines. They must recognize that only through continuous improvement will they achieve the defined quality that must be their goal.

If this is to occur, teachers must design lessons specifically addressing the learning actions (access, interpret, produce, disseminate and evaluate). Instruction on these learning actions will engage students in gathering and interpreting information so they can produce a product, service, or performance with their newly acquired insights and knowledge. Then they can disseminate or give their product, service, or performance to an authentic audience. They do all of these learning actions with a continuous focus on evaluating themselves and their work against the identified quality criteria that the teacher will be looking for.

The performance designer is a tool for teachers to use when planning for students to engage in a significant demonstration that is an interactive experience for students designed to include essential content, competence (learning actions), context (issue, situation, and audience), and quality criteria.

The completed performance designer will describe the total performance or demonstration of significance. All of the students' actions will be clearly stated. The teacher uses this performance designer to develop the necessary instructional sequences that will support the attainment of each of the desired actions. Once students know how to do the actions, they are ready to pursue the planned performance.

The following organizer provides an overview. Each major section in the planner is identified and corresponds to a detailed explanation that follows.

PERFORMANCE DESIGNER FORMAT

I

A PURPOSE	What complex thinking process is the focus?
B KEY ORGANIZING QUESTION	An issue or challenge to investigate.
C ROLE	You are _____ who is expected to ...

II

(Do what?)	(With what?)	(How well?)
D Access and **E** interpret by...	**F** CONTENT/CONCEPTS	**G** QUALITY CRITERIA "Look fors"

III

(In order to...)	(...do what?)	(How well?)
H Produce by...	**I** PRODUCT/ PERFORMANCE	**J** QUALITY CRITERIA "Look fors"

IV

	(To/for whom? where?)	(How well?)
K Disseminate by...	**L** AUDIENCE/ SETTING	**M** QUALITY CRITERIA "Look fors"

Section I

The first section of the designer serves as an organizer for the actions that follow.

PERFORMANCE DESIGNER ELEMENT	REFLECTIVE QUESTIONS
Ⓐ PURPOSE The reason the performance is worth doing. This section may be tied to state- or district-level assessment. It will more often relate to a complex thinking process that is the result of applied critical-reasoning skills. (Example: drawing a conclusion, making a recommendation.)	What do I want to be sure students are more competent doing when this performance is complete? Do I want them to be able to develop a range of possible solutions to a problem? Will they investigate an issue from outside school, form an opinion, or describe and support a point of view? What complex thinking skill is the core purpose of this performance?
Ⓑ KEY ORGANIZING QUESTION As with the purpose, the question focuses and organizes the entire performance. It combines with the role and the audience to define the context.	What will the students be accessing information about? Do I want to select the issue or question to be accessed, or will the students determine the learning they will pursue? Is the question or issue developmentally appropriate, and can I facilitate obtaining the resources that students will need for the issue? Do the students have any experiential background for this issue? Will the experience be limited to learning from the experiences of others?
Ⓒ ROLE When students take on a role, the point of view of the role adds a dimension not common to most learning. The role introduces the prompt that initiates the entire performance.	Will this role be authentic? Or is it a role-play? For example, students as artists, authors, and investigators are real roles for students. Students as lawyers, policemen, or city council members do not have the same level of authenticity. They would be role playing, which is pretending to be someone. Will there be more than one role or will students all be in the same role? How will I ensure that students will have a focused point of view to explore? In life outside school, who would answer this question or be concerned with this issue? What would that expert do? Who is the expert? What's the real role?

Section II

The second section of the performance designer focuses on having students carry out the learning actions of accessing and interpreting necessary content and concepts. The right-hand column of the top section defines the quality criteria, or "look fors," that will be taught, practiced, and assessed. These are the quality criteria of the performance benchmarks.

PERFORMANCE DESIGNER ELEMENT	REFLECTIVE QUESTIONS
Ⓓ ACCESS AND Accessing actions might require students to interview, locate, or read for information. The importance of student involvement in acquiring information requires a shift from teacher as information provider to teacher as facilitator for information accessing.	Where can information be accessed? Are there experts who can be interviewed? What publications will be helpful? Which texts contain related information? Who can we contact on the Internet? What other resources are available?
Ⓔ INTERPRET BY... *(Do what?)* Interpreting actions require students to review what they have collected and decide what it means now that they have it. Students may categorize the information they have, compare it with what they already know, and process it in a variety of critical and creative ways.	How will students interact with the information they have collected? Will they formulate new questions? Will they begin to be asked to draw conclusions or perhaps make predictions at this point in the performance? Who will students interact with to communicate their initial interpretations of the information? Will they have a peer conference? Will I ask questions or give answers?
Ⓕ CONTENT/CONCEPTS *(With what?)* This specifies the knowledge or information the students are to learn. The result at the end is only going to be as good as the information the students collect. The resources should go far beyond the text. The teacher should support with additional resources and literature examples.	What do the students need to know? Where will the information come from? What will be significant learning to retain after the performance is over? Why is it important for students to learn this? Where might they need to use it later? Next year? After they leave school? What connections can they make to other knowledge structures? What are different points of view?
Ⓖ QUALITY CRITERIA *("Look fors")* *(How well?)* Quality criteria are the specifications for the performance. It is critical that these "look fors" be observable and measurable and that they represent high-quality performances. The quality criteria stated in the third column will integrate the learning actions in the left-hand column with the content/concept to be learned in the center column.	What would an expert interviewer or artist do? What would be observable in the performance of a quality questioner or researcher? How would I know one if I saw one? Do the criteria match the learning action that has been selected and do they describe a logical and relevant application of the content/concept that is to be learned?

Section III

The third main section on the performance designer is organized similarly but focuses on the producing competence in the Learning Actions Wheel. The middle column of this section allows the teacher to describe or specify the nature of the product or performance the students are to generate. The right-hand column describes the quality criteria, or "look fors," that pertain to that product and production.

PERFORMANCE DESIGNER ELEMENT	REFLECTIVE QUESTIONS
⓱ PRODUCE BY... *(In order to...)* Producing actions ask students to synthesize their learning, to bring what has been learned together into a cohesive whole that has relevance. Students might design, build, develop, create, construct, or illustrate.	How will students bring what they have learned together? What actions will lead to a product and keep the students in the role? Are there stages to the producing action, such as design and develop or draft and write? What are the essential actions that will lead to a product?
⓲ PRODUCT/PERFORMANCE *(...do what?)* This describes the product, service, or production that the student will address. It should be something that will benefit the authentic audience.	What would an expert create? How does this product relate to the required or identified knowledge base? How does this product incorporate the required skills? What impact should the product have on the audience?
⓳ QUALITY CRITERIA *("Look fors")* *(How well?)* Quality criteria describe the learning actions as they occur in conjunction with the development of the product, service, or production. It is critical that the criteria be observable and measurable, and that it represent quality.	What would an excellent product look like? How could it be described? Will the product or production indicate the designing and developing that were used? How can it be precisely described in relationship to the learning actions? What are the essential actions the student will perform that relate to the producing verbs?

Section IV

The last section of the performance designer relates to the disseminating learning actions. It describes the sharing of the product. The middle column of this section clearly denotes the *audience* and the *setting*, or *context*, in which the performance will occur. These factors are critical in determining the realistic impact of the student's learning. The right-hand column will describe the quality criteria for this portion of the performance designer by combining the disseminating action in relationship with the authentic audience. It defines the purpose for the learning.

PERFORMANCE DESIGNER ELEMENT

REFLECTIVE QUESTIONS

PERFORMANCE DESIGNER ELEMENT	REFLECTIVE QUESTIONS
🄚 DISSEMINATE BY... Learning actions at this stage of the role performance or demonstration have the learners presenting their products, services, or productions. The form of the presentation will vary depending on the original purpose. The learner might disseminate by explaining, teaching, or dancing.	What will be the most efficient and effective form of communicating this new product? Will students choose to broadcast or publish or teach? How does this form best relate to the product and the purpose? How does this delivery relate to the role?
🄛 AUDIENCE/SETTING *(To/for whom? where?)* The audience will be the recipient of the learners' product or production. The degree of authenticity will be reflected in the composition of the audience. The setting for this performance could be related to the original issue being investigated as well as the purpose for this investigation, or the natural location of the recipient.	Who will benefit from the students' learning? Who can use this recommendation or this finding? Is it another learner? Someone at another grade level? Is it a team of engineers at General Motors? Or young patients in a dentist's office? Where is the audience?
🄜 QUALITY CRITERIA **"Look fors"** *(How well?)* The criteria describe the specification for delivering the product, service, or performance. They are observable and represent quality.	What does a quality presentation look like? What are the essential elements that clearly define a quality presentation? How do the criteria connect the disseminating actions with the learner and the audience?

The performance designer gives teachers a very useful tool for continuously defining learning in terms of a realistic role that students must either individually or collectively take on and accomplish. The performance designer also continuously engages students in the range of learning actions that successful people engage in after they graduate from school, but it does so in the safe environment of school under the careful guidance of the teacher. Learners will demonstrate each role performance according to their developmental level of growth. Continuous involvement and experience with learning actions and quality criteria will result in demonstrated student improvement and continuous upleveling of quality criteria that will fully prepare students for any performance benchmark they are asked to demonstrate.

EXAMPLES OF LEARNING ACTIONS

ACCESS:
Investigate
Gather
Interview
Research
Listen
Observe
Collect
Search
Inquire
Survey
View
Discover
Read
Explore
Examine

INTERPRET:
Analyze
Explain
Paraphrase
Rephrase
Clarify
Compare
Contrast
Summarize
Integrate
Evaluate
Translate
Prioritize
Synthesize
Sort
Classify

PRODUCE:
Create
Design
Develop
Draw
Write
Lay out
Build
Draft
Invent
Erect
Sketch
Assemble
Compose
Illustrate
Generate

DISSEMINATE:
Publish
Perform
Teach
Present
Transmit
Display
Explain
Broadcast
Act
Advertise
Discuss
Send
Sing
Dance
Telecast

EVALUATE:
Review
Reflect
Assess
Revisit
Compare
Conclude
Generalize
Prove
Question
Refute
Support
Verify
Test
Realign
Judge

SAMPLE PERFORMANCE DESIGNER FOR GRADE 3

PURPOSE:	MATHEMATICS:
To make and use measurements to solve problems	MEASUREMENT (SEE PAGE 43)

KEY ORGANIZING QUESTION:
How can I design a map others can use?

ROLE: *(You are ...)*
A map maker

(Who is expected to ...)

COMPETENCE (Do what?)	CONTENT/CONCEPTS (With what?)	QUALITY CRITERIA ("Look fors")
Access and interpret by ... exploring examining	simple maps and possible objects that could be used as nonstandard units of measure. locations on school grounds where you could plant a "treasure" (object to be located by others.	• Identifies nonstandard units of measure. • Compares nonstandard units of measure to standard units of measure. • Selects reasonable location to chart on map.

COMPETENCE (In order to ...	PRODUCT/PERFORMANCE ... do what?)	QUALITY CRITERIA ("Look fors")
Produce by ... designing and producing	a simple map for others to use to locate the "treasure" you have hidden on the school grounds.	• Plans location. • Produces clear, neat, symbols/drawings on map. • Includes simple legend for measurement. • Includes accurate measurement.

COMPETENCE	AUDIENCE / SETTING (To/for whom? where?)	QUALITY CRITERIA ("Look fors")
Disseminate by ... presenting	your map to another team in your class to see if they can follow it to your hidden "treasure."	• Explains treasure. • Provides others with copy of map. • Answers questions appropriately.

SAMPLE PERFORMANCE DESIGNER FOR GRADE 5

PURPOSE:
To make connections

MATHEMATICS:
NUMBER SENSE AND ESTIMATION
(SEE PAGE 17)

KEY ORGANIZING QUESTION:
How could you convince someone that numbers have multiple uses in the real world?

ROLE: *(You are ...)*
An author

(Who is expected to ...)

COMPETENCE *(Do what?)*	CONTENT/CONCEPTS *(With what?)*	QUALITY CRITERIA *("Look fors")*

Access and interpret by ...
 	
    investigating
 	
    analyzing
	the various ways numbers are used in daily life.
	
	the different types of mathematical use.
		• Identify what you are looking for.
		• Generate as many examples as possible.
		• Categorize your examples according to type of mathematical process used.

COMPETENCE *(In order to ...*	PRODUCT/PERFORMANCE *... do what?)*	QUALITY CRITERIA *("Look fors")*

Produce by ...
 	
    designing
 	
    creating
	a format for your book that includes various examples of how math is used in daily life. Explain why these uses are important.
	
	an illustrated book that depicts the important ways numbers are used in daily life.
		• Develop an outline for your book.
		• Organize the examples and explanations and illustrations according to types of mathematical processes.

COMPETENCE	AUDIENCE / SETTING *(To/for whom? where?)*	QUALITY CRITERIA *("Look fors")*

Disseminate by ...
    publishing
 	
    reading
	your book on *Mathematics in Daily Life.*
	
	it to a group of third-grade students.
		• Develop a plan for publishing your book.
		• Gather the necessary resources.
		• Produce the book.
		• Practice reading it for your audience.

SAMPLE PERFORMANCE DESIGNER FOR GRADE 8

PURPOSE:
To explore unit pricing and the concept of ratio

MATHEMATICS:
NUMERATION
(SEE PAGE 26)

- -

KEY ORGANIZING QUESTION:
How can customers use unit pricing to assist them when purchasing large portions?

- -

ROLE: *(You are ...)*
An investigative reporter

(Who is expected to ...)

COMPETENCE *(Do what?)*	CONTENT/CONCEPTS *(With what?)*	QUALITY CRITERIA *("Look fors")*
Access and interpret by ... researching analyzing	information on unit pricing at the local grocery store for at least 8 different items. your data to determine best value for the money spent.	• Identifies items and their unit cost. • Compares ratios accurately for those items. • Identifies best bargains for shoppers.

COMPETENCE *(In order to ...*	PRODUCT/PERFORMANCE *... do what?)*	QUALITY CRITERIA *("Look fors")*
Produce by ... designing	a shoppers' newsletter that recommends the best buys for shoppers. Justify your recommendations with relevant information.	• Includes pertinent and important information for shoppers. • Conveys information using standards of grammar and publishing.

COMPETENCE	AUDIENCE / SETTING *(To/for whom? where?)*	QUALITY CRITERIA *("Look fors")*
Disseminate by ... publishing and distributing	shoppers' newsletter to parents and other local citizens in the neighborhood.	• Develops a publishing plan. • Create a distribution plan. • Responds appropriately to any questions for more information.

SAMPLE PERFORMANCE DESIGNER FOR GRADE 12

PURPOSE:
To analyze a situation and create a framework

MATHEMATICS:
NUMBER SENSE AND ESTIMATION
(SEE PAGE 19)

KEY ORGANIZING QUESTION:
How can airline companies determine the best routes?

ROLE: *(You are ...)*
An advertising planner

(Who is expected to ...)

COMPETENCE *(Do what?)*	CONTENT/CONCEPTS *(With what?)*	QUALITY CRITERIA *("Look fors")*
Access and interpret by ... investigating analyzing	flight schedules and the cost of those flights from one major airline company. the gathered information to determine which flights might be offered to the public on sale.	• Gather necessary information from major airlines. • Compare and contrast the costs of flights into major cities. • Select the lights that would be financially beneficial for the airline and the customer. • Recommend sale schedule.

COMPETENCE *(In order to ...*	PRODUCT/PERFORMANCE *... do what?)*	QUALITY CRITERIA *("Look fors")*
Produce by ... designing and developing	a full-page newspaper advertisement for *USA Today* offering the flights you have selected for this promotional sale.	• Plan a full-page newspaper advertisement that clearly conveys information to the reader. • Clearly depict the advantages offered to the customer. • Communicate strong appeal.

COMPETENCE	AUDIENCE / SETTING *(To/for whom? where?)*	QUALITY CRITERIA *("Look fors")*
Disseminate by ... presenting defending	your ad to another team in your class. your choices and the logic behind those choices.	• Identifies focus and sticks to it. • Clearly explains the advantages to customer and airline. • Describes evidence that supports choices.

SAMPLE PERFORMANCE DESIGNER FOR GRADE 3

PURPOSE:
To make a recommendation

KEY ORGANIZING QUESTION:
How can your knowledge of numbers and your ability to estimate help you make decisions that will improve the conditions within your school?

ROLE: *(You are ...)*
An adviser to the PTA

(Who is expected to ...)

COMPETENCE *(Do what?)*	CONTENT/CONCEPTS *(With what?)*	QUALITY CRITERIA *("Look fors")*
Access and interpret by ... researching and analyzing	the number of chairs and tables needed to comfortably seat all of the students who stay for lunch.	• Identify your purpose. • Identify the needed data. • Select means for collecting the data. • Select the important pieces of information. • Calculate the best arrangement.

COMPETENCE *(In order to ...*	PRODUCT/PERFORMANCE *... do what?)*	QUALITY CRITERIA *("Look fors")*
Produce by ... designing and developing	a visual display showing the best arrangement. Include the necessary numbers.	• Identify your purpose. • Select your information. • Create a representation. • Include necessary accurate details.

COMPETENCE	AUDIENCE / SETTING *(To/for whom? where?)*	QUALITY CRITERIA *("Look fors")*
Disseminate by ... presenting and explaining	your chart and your recommendation to the PTA committee.	• Prepare and arrange your materials. • Rehearse your presentation with a real audience. • Make necessary changes • Deliver with clarity.

SAMPLE PERFORMANCE DESIGNER FOR GRADE 5

PURPOSE:

To solve a problem

- -

KEY ORGANIZING QUESTION:

How do artists and designers use mathematical patterns?

- -

ROLE: *(You are ...)*

A designer

(Who is expected to ...)

COMPETENCE *(Do what?)*	CONTENT/CONCEPTS *(With what?)*	QUALITY CRITERIA *("Look fors")*
Access and interpret by ... investigating and clarifying	how artists and designers use patterns and shapes when creating a mosaic. which shapes you would like to use. which shapes will work. what pattern you could try.	• Identify your purpose. • Select your resources. • Gather and record your data. • Select the most important information.

COMPETENCE *(In order to ...*	PRODUCT/PERFORMANCE *... do what?)*	QUALITY CRITERIA *("Look fors")*
Produce by ... designing and creating	a mosaic using geometric shapes. This mosaic would hang on the wall at the main entrance to the school.	• Identify your goal. • Choose appropriate shapes and materials. • Develop a sketch. • Determine a plan of action. • Make your mosaic.

COMPETENCE	AUDIENCE / SETTING *(To/for whom? where?)*	QUALITY CRITERIA *("Look fors")*
Disseminate by ... presenting and displaying	your completed mosaic at an assembly for your schoolmates.	• Organize the details and resources you plan to use. • Rehearse your presentation. • Change as necessary. • Use standard conventions for an audience.

SAMPLE PERFORMANCE DESIGNER FOR GRADE 8

PURPOSE:
To solve a problem and make a recommendation

MATHEMATICS:
GEOMETRY AND SPATIAL SENSE
(SEE PAGE 39)

KEY ORGANIZING QUESTION:
How would room size and shape affect the placement of video surveillance cameras?

ROLE: *(You are ...)*
An adviser for video camera placement

(Who is expected to ...)

COMPETENCE (Do what?)	CONTENT/CONCEPTS (With what?)	QUALITY CRITERIA ("Look fors")
Access and interpret by ... gathering analyzing	information on angles, distances, and lighting on the school stage. the gathered information in terms of possible camera placement and sweep action to fully record a skit that uses the whole stage.	• Identify the task carefully. • Measure and collect accurate data. • Record all collected data. • Consider all possibilities. • Select the locations that give full coverage with the least number of cameras.

COMPETENCE (In order to ...	PRODUCT/PERFORMANCE ... do what?)	QUALITY CRITERIA ("Look fors")
Produce by ... designing and creating	an accurately scaled visual representation including camera locations and areas and angles covered by each camera.	• Identify your purpose. • Create a draft. • Review for accuracy. • Refine as necessary. • Develop a final accurate product.

COMPETENCE	AUDIENCE / SETTING (To/for whom? where?)	QUALITY CRITERIA ("Look fors")
Disseminate by ... presenting and explaining	your accurately scaled diagram to the 10th-grade drama class.	• Select necessary information according to purpose. • Organize and rehearse. • Include specific details and defend decisions with facts. • Request feedback.

SAMPLE PERFORMANCE DESIGNER FOR GRADE 12

PURPOSE:
To solve a problem

KEY ORGANIZING QUESTION:
How can we use mathematics in designing and planning?

ROLE: *(You are ...)*
A problem solver

(Who is expected to ...)

COMPETENCE (Do what?)	CONTENT/CONCEPTS (With what?)	QUALITY CRITERIA ("Look fors")
Access and interpret by ... collecting and reviewing	all the necessary information and measurements needed to order carpet for the second floor of a house design that includes 3 bedrooms and 2 baths on the second floor.	• Identify your purpose. • Review possibilities. • Make a selection from several home designs. • Develop your data. • Select the important details.
then summarizing	all the measurements needed to place the order for the needed amount of carpet.	

COMPETENCE (In order to ...	PRODUCT/PERFORMANCE ... do what?)	QUALITY CRITERIA ("Look fors")
Produce by ... generating	an accurately scaled design of the rooms and hall to be carpeted. an order for the needed carpet (be sure to identify the width the carpet comes in).	• Apply your data to a scaled design of the area to be carpeted. • Create and order form that contains needed measurements. • Identify a specific carpet style and number.

COMPETENCE	AUDIENCE / SETTING (To/for whom? where?)	QUALITY CRITERIA ("Look fors")
Disseminate by ... presenting and discussing	with a local carpet salesperson.	• Organize your materials. • Establish a meeting time. • Record your interaction. • Review and respond to your performance.

APPENDIX: BLANK TEMPLATES

PERFORMANCE DESIGNER

PURPOSE:

- -

KEY ORGANIZING QUESTION:

- -

ROLE: *(You are ...)*

(Who is expected to ...)

COMPETENCE *(Do what?)*	CONTENT/CONCEPTS *(With what?)*	QUALITY CRITERIA *("Look fors")*
Access and interpret by ...		

COMPETENCE *(In order to ...*	PRODUCT/PERFORMANCE *... do what?)*	QUALITY CRITERIA *("Look fors")*
Produce by ...		

COMPETENCE	AUDIENCE / SETTING *(To/for whom? where?)*	QUALITY CRITERIA *("Look fors")*
Disseminate by ...		

Mathematics:
Grade ___

Performance
Benchmark

CONTENT/CONCEPT STANDARD ___

KEY ORGANIZING QUESTION:

KEY COMPETENCES	KEY CONCEPTS AND CONTENT	PERFORMANCE TASKS
		PERFORMANCE TASK I:
		PERFORMANCE TASK II:

QUALITY CRITERIA:

Technology Connections
_____: Grade ___

Performance Benchmark

KEY ORGANIZING QUESTION:

ACCESS	PRODUCE	DISSEMINATE
PERFORMANCE TASK I:	**PERFORMANCE TASK I:**	**PERFORMANCE TASK I:**
PERFORMANCE TASK II:	**PERFORMANCE TASK II:**	**PERFORMANCE TASK II:**

BIBLIOGRAPHY

Arizona Department of Education. (1992). *Arizona essential skills for mathematics.* Phoenix, AZ: Author.

Beane, J. A. (Ed.) (1995). *Toward a coherent curriculum, 1995 yearbook of the Association for Supervision and Curriculum Development.* Alexandria, VA: ASCD.

Burz, H. L. (1993, Winter). Getting started in the classroom with transformational outcome-based education. *Curriculum Technology Quarterly,* 1-2.

California State Department of Education. (1992). *Mathematics framework for California public schools, kindergarten through grade twelve.* Sacramento, CA: Author.

Coleman, W. (1993). *Educating Americans for the 21st century: A report of the National Science Board, Commission on Precollege Education in Mathematics, Science and Technology.* Washington, DC: National Science Board.

Covey, S. R. (1989). *The seven habits of highly effective people: Restoring the character ethic.* New York: Simon & Schuster.

Dossey, J. A., et al. (1988). *The mathematics report card: Are we measuring up?* Princeton, NJ: Educational Testing Service.

Durkin, D. (1978-1979). What classroom observation reveals about reading comprehension instruction. *Reading Research Quarterly, 4,* 482-534.

Gardner, H. (1985). *Frames of mind: The theory of multiple intelligence.* New York: Basic Books.

King, J. & Evans, K. (1991). Can we achieve outcome-based education? *Educational Leadership, 49* (2), 73-75.

Mathematical Sciences Education Board. (1991a). *Counting on you: Actions supporting mathematics teaching standards.* Washington, DC: National Academy Press.

Mathematical Sciences Education Board. (1991b). *For good measure: Principles and goals for mathematical measurement.* Washington, DC: National Academy Press.

Meiring, S. P. et al. (1992). *A core curriculum: Making mathematics count for everyone. Curriculum and Evaluation Standards for School Mathematics Addenda Series, Grades 9-12.* Reston, VA: National Council of Teachers of Mathematics.

Minnesota Department of Education. (1991). *Model learner outcomes for mathematics education.* St. Paul, MN: Author.

National Center for Education Statistics. (1991). *The state of mathematics achievement: NAEP's 1990 assessment of the nation and the trial assessment of the states.* Washington, DC: U.S. Department of Education.

National Center for Education Statistics. (1992). *The 1990 science report card: NAEP's assessment of fourth, eighth and twelfth graders.* Washington, DC: U.S. Department of Education.

National Council of Teachers of Mathematics. (1989). *Curriculum and evaluation standards for school mathematics.* Sacramento, CA: Author.

National Council of Teachers of Mathematics. (1991). *Professional standards for teaching mathematics.* Reston, VA: Author.

National Research Council. (1990). *Everybody counts: A report to the nation on the future of mathematics education.* Washington, DC: National Academy Press.

Senge, P. M. (1990). *The fifth discipline: The art and practice of the learning organization.* New York: Doubleday/Currency.

Spady, W. G. (1988). Organizing for results: The basis of authentic restructuring and reform. *Educational Leadership, 46*(2), 4-10.

Spady, W. G. (1994). *Outcome-based education: Critical issues and answers.* Arlington, VA: The American Association of School Administrators.

Spady, W. G., & Marshall, K. J. (1991). Beyond traditional outcome-based education. *Educational Leadership, 49*(2), 67-22.

Spady, W. G., & Mitchell, D. E. (1977). Competency-based education: Organizational issues and implications. *Educational Researcher, 6*(2), 9-15.

Spady, W. G., & Mitchell, D. E. (1978). Organizational contexts for implementing outcome-based education. *Educational Researcher, 7*(7), 9-17.

Steen, L. A. (1990). *On the shoulders of giants: New approaches to numeracy.* Washington, DC: National Academy Press.

Stenmark, J. K. (1991). *Mathematics assessment: myths, models, good questions and practical suggestions.* Reston, VA: National Council of Teachers of Mathematics.

U.S. Department of Education. (1991). *America 2000: An education strategy.* Washington, DC: Author.

Viadero, D. (1993, March 10). The coherent curriculum. *Education Week, 10-15.*

Virginia Polytechnic Institute and State University. (1992). *Kids and technology: Mission 21.* Albany, NY: Delmar.

CORWIN
PRESS

The Corwin Press logo — a raven striding across an open book — represents the happy union of courage and learning. We are a professional-level publisher of books and journals for K-12 educators, and we are committed to creating and providing resources that embody these qualities. Corwin's motto is "Success for All Learners."